It's NOT AS BAD AS IT LOOKS

Andy C Wareing

Andy C Wareing

CONTENTS

To Paula, my dear wife, best friend and adventurer

Love you always

Hockey Puck?

E vents had once more overtaken us. We had decided to return to the United States and had, again, set wheels to spin that had quickly become unstoppable. A mediocre burger in an oddly configured, too brightly lit pub had been the deal breaker. Our waitress had been young, sweet, and wildly incompetent, but that was fine. It had been the tasteless and arid burger that had pushed me over the edge. Well, now I seriously take the time to consider it, it was the combination of the hockey puck textured burger *and* the Suzuki Jimny car we had recently purchased.

Paula had fancied a Jimny since we had arrived back in the UK from our fateful attempt at a new life in Spain after moving from the USA. If you haven't read it yet, 'Mistakes Were Made' tells of that particular travel disaster. Anyway, a small four-wheel drive car to negotiate the narrow, winding, and boggy, mud-filled lanes of Somerset had sounded ideal. Large vehicles were a liability here and the Jimny was tiny in stature for sure. Designed around the footprint of a telephone box with a wheel at each corner, any acceleration had to be planned for a week or so in advance and even then, it had always found me wanting, white-knuckled with my right foot crushing the pedal to the floor.

In one attempt to join the busy M5 motorway, we found ourselves locked awkwardly eye to eye, for quite a while, with a trucker who was crawling down the slow lane beside us. He was tickled pink to see Paula and me rocking backward and forwards, flintstone-like, in our seats in a fruitless attempt to coax one more mile per hour than he, out of our tiny engine.

Everywhere we went we had the prestige of always being at the front of every traffic queue. Our box on wheels was like a tiny little grey parade leader, we would always be at the head of any procession of infuriated motorists on any road that had the very slightest of inclines.

It was in the Jimny we had driven to the Drayton Crown Public House and Hotel that weary night in November, just prior to the winter Covid lockdown that Boris would soon enact. The night was cold and Somerset dark. The single lanes were all unlit and winding and the hedgerows, even in Winter, were so tall that it felt like driving through a tunnel. The wipers carefully rearranged the rainwater on the windscreen into a blinding smear, and even with the heater on full blast, we were forced to clear small portholes in the condensation with increasingly damp elbows, through which we could peer, squint-eyed, into the dark night ahead of us. I checked several times that I had actually turned the headlights on, they illuminated the wet roads ahead with slightly less than half the brilliance of an usherette's torch.

To maximize the power of the meager engine, such luxuries as temperature gauges and navigational aids had been left out of the Jimny's design. It didn't even have a clock; I guess because Suzuki assumed that the type of person who buys a Jimny isn't too worried about what time of day they might eventually arrive; a calendar would have been of more use. There *was* a radio in the dashboard and an aerial on the roof but we never managed to get more than a hiss of static from the speakers no matter which knobs we twirled.

We parked the car and I soaked my socks in a vast puddle that had been left there for the use of visiting guests. The hand sanitizer at the entrance was of a disconcerting consistency that refused to either be rubbed in or wiped off; the waiting area by the hostess's stand was filled with people holding out hands wetly away from posh frocks and dress jackets while we all exchanged awkwardly embarrassed British grins.

The pub section of the Drayton was lovely. Just what you expect from a rural 16th-century country coaching house. Broad oak beams traced the ceiling, horse brasses twinkled in the flickering flames of the vast wood fire in the corner opposite the long oak bar, and the cheerful voices and hushed laughter from the patrons ensconced deep in their comfortable leather armchairs were charming. Unfortunately, the dining room was next door, and for some peculiar reason, the owners had decided to decorate it like a 1990s bus station waiting room. Plain beige wallpaper, small framed modern art, and hard angular furniture worked effectively together as charm extractors.

Truth be told, it wasn't the burger or the Jimny or even the hard lip of the plastic chair that bit into my buttocks that really made us both reconsider life in the UK. It was the awful combination of choices taken from us and our desperately missing Adam.

The plan had always been to retire from the express lane that is corporate America to a sun-drenched and pocket-friendly life by the Mediterranean. When the pandemic ruined that dream, we sought refuge in the UK. In Somerset to be precise, which was lovely and rural, but very quiet and without a warm azure ocean to fall asleep beside. And of course, without Adam. Adam our younger adult son, who had accompanied us on that crazy drive through Europe and played 'bitty batty' by the villa's pool with us and made us laugh and cry in equal measures. He had returned to the USA to restart his old life with his old friends, and I think we were both a little lost without him.

We decided on a hard reset. Go back to the USA and see what another few years in the sunshine would hold for us. It was likely we would return to Somerset in a few years, but it would be at a time of our choosing. And we would get to spend some time with Adam and maybe even Ben, if we managed to get back in time before he was deployed with the US Navy to Japan.

A Somerton Xmas

We made it back to Tetsworth to see Kaz and Steve, Paula's sister and brother-in-law in early December, just a few days before Boris Johnson's infamous Christmas lockdown U-Turn. The government's plan had been to relax existing COVID restrictions over the Christmas period and allow people to celebrate five days of family mixings of up to three households. People assumed that this guidance had been well considered and went out to purchase food to share and family gifts to disperse accordingly. Then, on the morning of the 20th of December, the government canceled Christmas.

It would only become apparent many months later, that while ordinary Brits canceled their get-togethers once more, for the benefit and health of the greater good, Boris Johnson and many like him in his government partied in Number 10 like there was literally no tomorrow.

The Jimny had got us safely to Tetsworth and back, although it needed frequent stops at petrol stations in both directions. Traffic was amazingly light for us; we didn't see a single car in front of us the entire way. Unfortunately, one quick and furtive glance in the rearview mirror revealed that we had single-handedly created the longest conga line of traffic in the history of the southwest as we slowly scaled the long uphill section of the A303 close to Stonehenge. A traffic news helicopter buzzed alongside us the entire way, kindly giving other road users updates on where we would likely create the next major traffic incident.

Back in Somerton, in our little rental cottage, we prepared for a lockdown Christmas. We bought a massive leg of lamb and bags of carrots, sprouts, and beans for twenty pence a bag each. Twenty pence! How do the farmers prepare and sow the fields, tend the crops, fertilize and control pests, harvest the crops, clean and pack and then ship them to the supermarkets to get them onto our shelves for twenty pence? Paula and I still marvel at that feat.

We bought a tiny Christmas tree from Overt Locke on Somerton High Street and a string of LED lights to decorate, all for fifteen pounds. Overt Locke is one of those old and traditional hardware stores. It sells EVERYTHING. I mean it, seriously. There is stuff in there from the day it was opened in 1925. Garden fencing, mobility trolleys, bolts and screws of every type and dimension, egg cups, beer brewing kits, everything. I have never visited and come away disappointed.

I had life-size head and shoulder pictures of the kids printed on cardboard and gave them, wrapped, to Paula as gifts on Christmas morning. We opened our few presents to each other while we listened to the bells of St. Michaels and All Angels call the faithful for morning services. We posed for selfies with the pictures of the 'kids' taped to their dining chairs while we ate our lamb dinner. With Christmas done, we fell asleep watching the usual Christmas drivel on the TV.

On New Year's morning, we got up before dawn and walked to the fields to see the sun rise above the empty fields. It was frosty, and the spider's webs created sparkling intricate drapes that hung in the gaps between the iron railings by the cemetery. There was no sign of the sunrise, a thick mist lay over the fields and the sun was entirely obscured, but it was a nice way to start 2021 regardless.

We walked the pups, Archie and Pi, along our favorite bridleway each day. There are an astonishing 140,000 miles of protected paths open to the public in the UK. They are maintained by the local councils and supported by the National Trust and the Countryside Charity. They provide public access even across privately owned farmland and provide amazing walks all across Great Britain. Be aware though that these 'rights of way' are not universally liked by the farmers who own the land, and there is nothing to stop a disgruntled farmer from sticking a virile and pointy-horned one-ton bull in the field you need to cross to complete your trip.

Between April 2020 and March 2021, eleven people were killed by cows and bulls. Six of the deaths were caused by cattle, and five by bulls. Farmers and landowners *are* required to demonstrate a reasonable duty of care to others. Earlier in 2021 one farmer received a suspended prison sentence and a hefty fine after 83-year-old David Tinniswood was trampled to death and his wife seriously injured when they were walking on a footpath that passed through the yard of a farm. They were accompanied by their two border terriers. The couple was attacked by cattle that were grazing in the field with calves at foot.

There are 9.8 million head of cattle in the UK and while the focus of blame is often leveled at bulls, it is the suckling herds that cause the most conflict with the walking public. These suckling herds are mothers with young calves and many incidents are caused by whole herd attacks, not a single animal, as the mothers act on their hormone-fueled instincts to protect their offspring. The most dangerous combination appears to be when walker, dog, and suckling cow end up in the same field.

The hazard is somewhat aggravated by how the NFU plays the danger down. One spokesperson recently offered this advice, "just take a walking stick ...be bold and walk straight through them."

And the media, predictably, only offers statistics based on mortalities for obvious reasons. But cow attacks are frightening and occur much more often than they are reported. A BBC publication from 2014 provides average annual figures of roughly 3 deaths, 40 serious injuries, and 37 lesser injuries. What they do not discuss is that all of these 80 annual incidents had the *potential* to be fatal. A quarter ton of beef on the hoof can charge at close to twenty-five miles an hour and can quickly become a scene from Pamplona when accompanied by her stompy udder buddies.

The advice for dealing with an attack from cattle is about as consistent as that given to folks faced by bears. Don't run, but if you have to run, run downhill. Stand tall and wave your arms. Punch one on the nose—yes, that's real advice. As Jim Gaffigan said in one of his routines "I don't know, guys. The whole 'play dead when a bear attacks' thing sounds suspiciously like something the bears would come up with..."

The best advice given is to simply not enter a field that contains cows.

On one of our walks, a cold January day with a strong and bitter wind that blew out of the east and brought a flurry of snowflakes to sweep in an almost horizontal curtain across the fields, we stumbled on a young couple having a picnic. Sat in the mud and swaddled in thick coats and bobble hats they were sharing scotch eggs and something steaming out of a tartan thermos flask. As we passed, the couple looked up as though they had been caught in some secret assignation. Both looked guilty and concerned.

"Hiyah," we both said as friendly as we could.

"Oi Oi," said the young chap looking up with cheeks flushed red by the scathing wind. This strange greeting is what we colloquially use in these here Somerset parts of the UK to mean, "Hello there, good fellow, I hope all is well with you and yours?"

We walked away and then, suitably separated by a reasonable distance fell about laughing at the weirdness and outright Britishness of the situation. The day was ghastly, one only suitable to quickly walk the dogs and then head back indoors for tea and jam-covered toast, while toes were warmed by a roaring fire. I thought it was so funny I tried to secretly take a picture of them with my iPhone so that I could post it on Facebook later to amuse our American friends, but the distance was too great, so we just carried on with our walk.

On the way back the couple had disappeared. It was only then that we took time to realize that they were indeed meeting in secret. Covid restrictions meant that people from different households were not allowed to meet, and when they unexpectedly saw us in the lane, they almost certainly thought they had been rumbled. Stupid me even tried to take a picture of them and they had scarpered, probably thinking we had called the police on them. Bloody Covid.

Anyway, back to the cottage for tea and toast and to plan our move back to the USA.

FACEBOOK MARKETPLACE

B elieve it or not, we were getting really good at this international moving business. We knew how to get the dogs back into the USA and, we had the added advantage that going back to the States, the entire process is way easier than getting them moved from the USA to anywhere in Europe. We found a company that would supply packing boxes and all the customs forms and do a door-to-door delivery of our few earthly possessions. All we needed now was a door to send them to.

We spent some considerable time looking at where in the USA we would want to be. Denver, Seattle, or somewhere in Florida? In the end, we decided one of the main reasons to go back was to be near Adam, so we decided to just return to Atlanta. We also knew that our old subdivision was still popular, with houses selling fast and for premium prices. If we ever decided to come back to the UK, we would be able to sell relatively quickly. With that in mind, we began to look to see what was on the market, in or close to where we had last sold less than a year ago.

Nothing was the answer. Inventory everywhere in Atlanta was devastatingly low. Covid continued to suppress home sales and most homes were selling off the market and for above asking price. Every day we would trawl the markets and Realtor.com to see if anything new had become available. It was all a little depressing, there was just nothing new out there.

Then a stroke of luck. We pinged some folks in our old neighborhood on Facebook to see if anybody knew of any houses coming up for sale and we got a response. A neighbor we slightly knew had been thinking of moving but hadn't listed yet. They would think about it and get back to us. A few days later we bought a house, sight unseen with the exception of a few old photographs, with most of the transactions, everything except the legal contracts really, all done on Facebook.

We set a date of April 30th for flights back to ATL and then started the mad panic to sell and/or ship our all of goods.

Life is funny. You spend day after day, especially in COVID lockdowns, watching them slip slowly by, kicking the tin can of daily chores down the pavement of a humdrum life. Then you decide, once more, to move countries and time suddenly accelerates, spinning away in a Coriolis of wastewater down a chortling drain. Days suddenly streaked by. Paula, as always, efficiently organized the dog's flights. We shipped some boxes to our new address, you know the one, the house we hadn't actually yet seen, to be stored for us in the garage. We gave notice on the rental that we would be forced to break our lease a few months early. Luckily, they had a new tenant who wanted to move in earlier, if at all possible, so we agreed to mutually terminate.

In between the panic of shipping and organizing flights and setting up the US house remotely, the shape of the pandemic took a marked shift and the effect was immediately noticeable in the village. On 8 December 2020, 90-year-old Margaret Keenan received a Pfizer-BioNTech vaccine at University Hospital in Coventry. The first one in the UK. Soon after, the roll-out of the vaccine to at-risk, care home residents and their carers, and those over eighty years of age followed.

Prior to the vaccine roll-out, the streets of Somerton were mostly deserted. The older population prudently avoided everybody. When forced to venture from their homes to top up on supplies of Steradent denture cleaner, Anusol arse cream, and three slices of thinly sliced haslet, you would find them fully masked, huddled in shop doorways and stepping recklessly into the street to avoid passersby.

By the middle of January, the streets were a sea of grey nodding heads, catching up on a year's worth of gossip, they huddled together in packs of taupe anoraks amid circled wagons of tartan granny trolleys outside the supermarket, forcing others, many still waiting for their vaccinations, to step into the street to avoid them.

On our regular walk across the fields, the lanes were always empty. On one sunny morning in February, we were surprised to find the lane filled with a sea of shuffling shambling bodies, a veritable scene from a popular Atlanta-based zombie TV series.

In February I received a text from the NHS asking me to schedule my first vaccination, so we drove to Dillington House country estate where I queued in the frosty air for thirty minutes, rolled up a sleeve, and received my first dose of, what millions in the United States believed to be Bill Gates's secretive microchip serum, otherwise known in the UK (and most of the rest of the world) as the Pfizer-BioNTech COVID-19 Vaccine. Paula had to wait several weeks for hers and by the time her appointment rolled around only Moderna was available.

Funny though, I did start to receive a lot more emails about Windows updates, and they always knew where I was.

All of a sudden, we were only four days away from our flights back to the USA. Kaz and Steve had hired a van and would arrive on Friday to spend the night with us, say goodbye, and take some of our things they wanted back to Tetsworth. We booked our COVID tests in a Boots pharmacy in Taunton, and an hour later arranged with a car buying company to drive to their premises and exchange the Jimny for a check of similar proportions to the car itself.

We spent the evening with Kaz and Steve and waved our goodbyes on Saturday morning. Now all we had left to do was to clean the rental cottage and wait for our COVID test results and the pet courier to show up to collect the dogs.

Archie and Pi had to stay in kennels close to Heathrow the night before their flight back to the US. We had decided to spend the night close to Heathrow ourselves. It was nearly a three hours' drive back to the Airport and we honestly weren't sure what to expect at security so we wanted to be there ready for our flight.

The dogs were picked up in the morning by a lovely chatty fellow. We gave the pups hugs and kisses and said our farewells. Nothing we could do now, they were on their way, and soon, so would we be. The courier fellow promised to call us later when he arrived at the overnight facility and so, with a sigh, we watched them drive through the gates and disappear once more from view.

The COVID tests thankfully came back negative as we waited for our taxi. Delta was trialing a new app that, in theory at least, allowed travelers to upload the results of tests and submit them electronically to the airline. I couldn't get it to work, it just refused to accept the UK test results so I abandoned trying. It was labeled as a trial only and wasn't mandatory for travel so we didn't think about it again. I had printed all of the paperwork off anyway just to be certain.

We spent the night in the airport concourse at an Aerotel. It was typically COVID-esque, like a large and abandoned shell of its former self. A vast and entirely empty dining hall, a bar shuttered and closed and barely a body to be seen. Even the main doors to the hotel had been abandoned and we had to ring a doorbell by a side door. It gave the mundane task of hotel check-in the same fission of excitement that 1930s Chicagoans must have felt when seeking ingress to an illicit speakeasy in the height of prohibition, "knock twice and ask for Harry."

We found a wonky trolley for our towering pile of cases and the two lads, neither of whom resembled anybody who might be called Harry, who was on reception, checked us in and then watched, without interest or the motivation to help, as we struggled to get the trolley and ourselves simultaneously into the cramped and quickly closing elevator.

The room was crowded, especially with five large cases and two backpacks, and was entirely windowless. But the beds were crisp and clean and the bathroom was sparkling. We had brought sandwiches and snacks, as we knew the only food available was likely to be the extortionately priced pot noodle in the hotel lobby vending machine. As we settled in, Paula got a call from the dog guy. Pi and Archie had arrived safe, had some food and water and a walk around the fenced and safe compound, and were, like us, hunkering down for our last night in the UK.

O SAY CAN YOU SEE...

Morning brought trepidation and worry for us all. Pi and Archie would be heading to the airport. They had with them all of the paperwork that needed to be in order for them to fly, but they had slipped far from our circle of care and control and we had our own concerns, security to clear, and a plane back to Atlanta to catch.

It was a short walk from the hotel to the pandemonium of the terminal. Considering only US nationals were allowed to return to the USA at that time, and Delta was still restricting seating to create spacing between passengers, it was startling busy. The reason soon became apparent. Heathrow security staff must have received a memo about the new Delta COVID testing app and rather than interpret the use of the app as a 'trial', as was clearly stated on the Delta website, they had viewed it as a mandatory requirement for travel. If travelers hadn't uploaded their results, they needed to step out of line, install the new app, and scan their paperwork. I had the app installed but our English results, sent electronically by our local testing center, still refused to synch with the Delta app which I am certain had only ever been tested within the USA. It might have worked with a test result obtained from Walgreens or CVS, but I suspect the app developers hadn't quite gotten around to testing it with the output from a little Boot's chemist shop on Taunton High Street.

We were finally called forward after explaining the situation, the same situation the majority of traveling passengers were in, given we had all taken tests in the UK so that we could travel back to the US. The seventeen-year-old security person gave me an angry and embittered stare and with a shake of his head tried to scan our Boot's results himself. Nothing happened so he tried again and then, finally, waved us through so that the desk clerk could read through our results on the hard paper copies I had printed out.

There were a few shops open selling perfume and sandwiches, a huge improvement from when we had arrived in June the year before, but it was still quiet, so we bought some bottles of water for the flight and walked slowly to the gate and found some empty seats.

The flight back to the US was without incident. It felt good to be going 'home', even though a new house we had yet to see awaited us. But Adam was in town and we would hopefully see him later for dinner. The timing from other perspectives was not great. We had missed our eldest son, Ben, by a mere week or so. He had flown through Atlanta, but then immediately caught another flight to Seattle, and from there onward to Tokyo to start his new posting in the US Navy. With Japan entirely locked down, it didn't seem likely we would see him for some considerable time.

We landed in ATL and piled our luggage on another wonky-wheeled trolley. Outside in the familiar dazzling sunshine and humidity-heavy air stood our old friend and neighbor Bob, who had dropped us off at the same curbside less than a year ago so that we could start our fateful journey to Spain.

Time is a trickster, isn't she? Most assuredly the ultimate deceiver of our frail human recollections and experiences. We had said farewell to Bob on June 17th, 2020, and here we were back again on the first day of April 2021. The pages and pencil-squiggled entries on our calendar assured us that only nine scant months and a handful of days had passed, but that's not what our minds and memories informed. In our minds, the road trip across France to Spain had been a journey of several months in and of itself. Surely, we had lived and endured the becalmed quietude of life in Spain and the villa for a year, maybe two, and then life back in England, our escape from COVID and the insanity of international border closings was another series of passing months marked only by the many changing English seasons.

How many birthdays had I celebrated since we left? Three, four perhaps? But that just couldn't be right...right? I had celebrated only one birthday and that was back in Somerton in September before Adam had returned to the US. Then one fleeting autumn, a short, mild winter, and the very beginnings of a flowery spring had passed us by. Too many experiences, good and bad, in too short a time to process, I guess. Unbelievable.

We drove north up I-85, passed the gleaming dome of City Hall covered in gold extracted from the mines in Dahlonega, passed the iconic (in Atlanta anyway) towers of Sun Trust Plaza and Bank of America Plaza, the rotating restaurant of the Westin Peachtree Plaza and then we passed the twin buildings that everybody who traveled north of the perimeter called the King and Queen buildings due to the white lattice 'crowns' that adorned them.

And then, there we were, parked up in the drive of the house we had bought on Facebook.

REUNITED

The house was both what we expected and in many ways a mixture of surprises. The back garden was much larger than it had appeared in the photographs the seller had sent across to us. Both larger and more overgrown. Unlike most of the houses in the neighborhood, it had been left largely untouched since the house had been built in the late 1980s. Massive pine trees towered into the sky, blocking all light from reaching the ground. The earth had become arid and only tussocks of weed caressed the hill that sloped upwards and away from the house. It was clear that we also had a drainage problem. From the right of the property, a deep gully had been carved across the entire back of the house from the heavy rains.

In fact, the photographs of the house we had been sent, had been rather selectively used. The garage was large but was crowded with kitchen units that we assumed had been moved when the kitchen had been updated. It was useful storage for sure, but it meant there was no way to get two American cars in there. We opened a couple of the cupboard doors and found innumerable tins of paint, stacked high, ancient, and half-used. It was customary to leave some paint that could be used to touch up the interior walls and external siding, but none of these matched any of the current house colors, and there was a huge pile of the bloody things.

The kitchen and living room were nice, in need of paint but habitable. The spare bedrooms were a disgrace. Decorated by teenage girls, the closet doors were still covered in a splurge of blackboard paint and every wall bristled like a porcupine with all of the thumbtacks and nails that must have held up pictures of celebrities. Much of the sheetrock required patching and everything needed a repaint.

The worst by far was the master bathroom. It was still original, from when the house was built. It was dated, with cracked tiles in the shower, a decrepit tub, and discolored, yellow grout between the cheap white subway tiles. All of the faucets were stained and rusting, loose in their fittings. We ran the faucet and the tub slowly filled with rust-colored water from the failing water heater in the garage. Paula gave the lightest of touches to the Venetian blind and with a loud clatter, the entire thing fell to the ground at her feet. It must have been held up, only by the useless prayers of the previous occupants.

We had only ourselves to blame I guess, but it was disappointing that we now faced a major renovation before the master bath was really usable. Part of the reason to move back to the USA was to see if we had sufficient funds to put a private pool into the yard. It was still possible, but the state of the yard itself and the unforeseen costs of the additional renovations would eat into our budget considerably.

The sound of the doorbell interrupted our initial dismay. The dogs had finally arrived. They were exhausted and dehydrated but immensely happy to see us, and we them. We got them out of their crates and they bounced around wanting to greet us both at the same time. We got a massive bowl of cold water and they spent the next five minutes in the air conditioning, spreading water across the floors of the kitchen. That's when Adam rolled up and we had to repeat the whole greeting over, except this time Pi jumped up a little too vigorously into Adam's face and split his lip.

We walked across the road to Vintage Pizza for dinner, Adam dabbing the blood from his mouth on a handkerchief. Entering the restaurant was immensely disconcerting. The sudden press of bodies, the clattering of glasses, and the scrape of knives and forks on plates were only overpowered by the background hubbub of human voices. For the first few minutes, we were entirely overwhelmed.

In both Spain and England, for the entire time we were there, all that we had really experienced was lockdown. The pubs had opened for a week here and there but even when they did, social distancing and one-way traffic had been implemented, and not many people wanted to take the risk of socializing anyway. Supermarkets were quiet and people just generally avoided mixing with people outside of their own households.

The very polar opposite was true here. Vintage Pizza was packed. After months of avoiding people, or having the government forcing us to do so, we were suddenly immersed into a throng, diners and servers, elbow to elbow, laughing, coughing, shouting, sneezing, drinking beers, sharing pizza slices as big as entire dinner plates and patting each other on the backs. It was as if COVID had passed the USA by, which by the yardstick of infection and death rates it absolutely had not. But by pure unwillingness to alter the behavior of their everyday American lives, the pandemic had largely gone unnoticed and the crisis that gripped the rest of the world had been marked firmly as 'over'.

Funny though, some cold beer and a pizza with enough salty meat to make me clutch my left arm later, we were right there, back in the groove with them. It was the best feeling seeing Adam again. He had settled straight back into his old life, renting an apartment not that far from us with his old friend Bob (real name Mike – I have no idea, don't even ask). We spent a few hours together catching up on each other's stories and news, and finally, as exhausted as our pups were, we said farewell to him. We watched his black Mazda drive off into an evening filled with the familiar and comforting sounds of cicadas and rumbling thunder and went back into this strangely unfamiliar house we now owned.

Bob and his wife Becky had done us proud. They had provided their small travel fridge and filled it with cold beers and milk. Tea and bread were stacked on the kitchen tops along with sanitary wipes and soap. They had even assembled some patio furniture we had ordered and shipped to the house. Upstairs we all collapsed onto the still slowly inflating mattress Bob had kindly dragged up the stairs for us in preparation for our arrival.

The next day, somewhat refreshed, we borrowed a car from our lovely neighbor Trish and drove to CarMax. Everybody in the USA knows and loves, or hates, CarMax. But readers from countries where you still have to negotiate car prices with oily dealers dressed in sheepskin coats, caricatures like Swiss Tony and Boycie, they are a Godsend.

There are two-hundred-and-twenty-five CarMax superstores in the USA, twelve in Georgia alone. The concept is to do the business of car selling and buying differently. A typical CarMax store is 59,000 square feet and positively brims over with an inventory of around 400 vehicles. Each car goes through a thorough 125-point inspection process, far beyond any state-required inspections, and includes a 90-day warranty and a 30-day money-back guarantee. There is zero negotiation for either buying or selling. The sticker price is what you pay for a car, and the on-site appraisal price of your vehicle is what you get, there and then, if you are willing to sell. In and out within the hour. The original name for the concept was 'Honest Rick's Used Cars,' which I like immensely.

The best bit is that on the lot, all of the doors of the 400 cars are open, so you can walk around without a salesperson hassling you and sit in all of the vehicles you like. Open the boot, reconfigure the seats, estimate how much shopping and/or dogs would fit in the space, press all of the buttons on the dash, and honk every horn, all without speaking to anybody. On the occasional rainy day in Atlanta, we would drive to our nearest CarMax and just spend the day, walking around the lot, Paula sitting in all of the SUVs and me sitting in all of the Porsches, one hand on the steering wheel and the other on the gear knob, making VRUMMM—BRUMMM noises to myself.

Not so on this visit. The vast lot was mostly empty. The global silicon chip shortage meant new vehicles were, for the greatest part, unavailable. Secondhand cars were in demand and choices were few. Luckily, clever Paula had reserved a bright blue Ford Escape and it was there waiting for us. We sat in it, opened all the doors, reconfigured the seats, pressed some random buttons on the dash, etc. etc., and then went into the office space to arrange a test drive. That's when I realized that I no longer held valid US insurance. Normally, we could test drive using the CarMax corporate umbrella insurance as long as the salesperson drove along with us, but that was no longer allowed due to COVID. I made some phone calls to the insurance agent who insured the house but that path proved too costly and tricky. That's when we remembered the 30-day guarantee. If we paid for the car in full, we could drive it off the lot and return it for a full refund nearly a month later if we didn't like it. Way cheaper than a rental car! Deal done.

JABS & SHADY

The next few weeks were spent catching up with friends in the neighborhood and more importantly, consuming all of the American food we had missed. We ate a factory farm full of buffalo wings with fries and ranch dressing at Taco Mac. We had 16oz steaks at Outback, medium rare thank you, with Aussie fries and all washed down with big bloke Stella Artois in ice-crusted glasses. We met Adam for a chilled beer on the patio of Marlowe's Tavern next to the Pike Nursery, and without caring to look at the menu, ordered Royale's with cheese, a wagyu beef burger cooked to greasy perfection and topped with pickle and that type of bright yellow American cheese that will melt but refuse to ever set again. And we had a mercury blood poisoning amount of sushi wherever and whenever we could.

We drove to see Adam's apartment in Sandy Springs. It was really nice, tidy, and large with a massive corner patio that overlooked the communal pool. Both Paula and I independently checked his bathroom to make sure he had deodorant and toothpaste, and, happy that he possessed the minimum requirements of adulthood, bought him a dispiriting lunch across the road at North River Tavern.

In England, we had only had time to receive part one of the two-part COVID vaccination, and we wanted to keep our options to travel open, so we booked another at Walgreens. The rush had died down by the time we arrived and you could book your two slots at any convenient time, in any of the tens of pharmacies that surrounded us.

We knew from previous history that the USA had zero interest in what jabs you had accrued in other countries. When the kids signed up to enter the US school system fifteen years ago, we brought all of their vaccination histories with us, carefully printed out by our local GP on letterheaded surgery paperwork and signed by their doctor. It mattered not a jot. They were re-vaccinated with everything they had already received in the UK.

The best way forward was to ignore the first COVID jab we had received in England and simply start again. A couple of weeks later we had shots two and three. Now over-vaccinated, but with the all-important proof, printed on our little Walgreen cards we felt safe(er) to circulate amongst the general population.

We sat patting our tender arms that night as we ate Thai delicacies at M Thai Street Food on the Alpharetta Highway. On the way home I realized we were really close to where we had initially taken shelter while we waited for the international flights to resume, all that long time ago back in June of 2020. I drove the car slowly down Shady Grove Lane. Many of these old, but pleasant and well-maintained homes were now up for sale. The development of Downtown Alpharetta had been a rampant success. After a decade or more of Americans neglecting their local shops, instead expressing a preference to drive twenty miles further to shop in a soulless, artificially climate-controlled mall and dine in a noisy crowded food court like seagulls around a waste bin full of discarded fries, the novel concept of 'walkable living' had returned.

It began for us folks who lived on the Alpharetta/Milton border with the creation of Avalon, an eighty-six-acre 'community' of shops, dining, hotel, office spaces, and eight hundred studio apartment-type homes. Never mind that the only shops on offer were mostly high-end designer outlets that displayed a total of three shirts and a silky neckerchief all staffed by models with eating disorders and a sour expression that screamed "you can't afford to shop here". There is also an Apple store and a Tesla dealership. Despite these obvious limitations to a happy shopping experience, the crowds flocked.

I just didn't get it. Growing up in the UK you are used to a local network of small independent businesses, the butcher, the baker, the...well come to think about it...I think he might have gone out of business. Not to say that in the UK the big guns aren't doing their best to eradicate the high street. Tesco's, Asda, and Morrisons, they all lurk on any massive patch of industrial land on the outskirts of any decent-sized urbanization, tempting shoppers to save two pence on a tin of beans or a penny on a loaf. And I'm certainly not such a hypocrite to suggest for one second that we don't shop at them, those savings are way too good. But we also buy all of our bacon and sausages from the butcher just across the road, bread and cakes from our baker, and wine, magazines, and sweets from our 'open all hours' type newsagents.

In Avalon, the whole thing is entirely false. The streets don't go anywhere, their sole raison d'être is to whisk you from one purse-emptying experience to the next. The facades of the buildings are designed to make you think you are in a living and breathing town, a community, but all they do is screen you from the gargantuan car park and expressway that delivers new buying blood to the outlets it contains.

They even pipe in Christmas music and spray false snow onto the synthetic ice rink from October onwards. Here is part of the blurb from the website:

"Avalon infuses resort-level hospitality throughout a walkable, seamlessly connected community of shopping, dining, entertainment, living, and working. It's more than just another place to go, it's a place to be — a hub of activity that delivers the luxury of the modern South."

HURRRP. I think I just threw up a little in my mouth.

It was so popular, so quickly, that all of a sudden, our local Mall on North Point fell into financial trouble. When its anchor store, Sears closed its doors, its doom was sealed.

The same has happened in downtown Alpharetta. A new school, a boutique hotel, a smattering of expensive, but not very good restaurants, and heaps of premium living had created a bizarre and eclectic mix of what corporate America had insidiously informed, and convinced, middle-class Americans it craved. With tables and chairs cluttering the sidewalks, diners, in the heat and humidity of the South, sweat into their Caesar salads and drink warm ten-dollar wheat micro brews through gritted teeth.

As a result, all of the reasonably priced family houses in the area had been snapped up by developers. Not to be improved, as the profit margins in that would be too meager, but to be torn down and million-dollar mansions erected on their foundations.

And so, it was with our little ranch house on Shady Grove Lane, the house we had rented for a few months. We had painted it and planted flowers in the window boxes, fixed the leaky faucets, put up our pictures and chased the cockroaches and snakes into the neighbor's yard. We parked up outside now.

There was nothing left but the concrete path that used to lead up to our front door, but now, forlornly, led only to a massive hole in the barren russet earth. A yellow digger with its shovel raised into the air silently saluted the blue and hopefully vacant chemical toilet that teetered on the crater's edge. We knew the demolition was going to happen, the owner had told us as much when we signed the lease, and it was just a rental home, but for some strange reason we were all blissfully happy there and it jangled the nerves somehow to see it gone, and all of the neighboring homes soon to share its fate.

Oh No, Not Todd Again

We built a pagoda on the back of the house and I got up early to pound sand and lay concrete pavers before the Georgia sun had a chance to break from the cover of the trees and send my pale English body scattering in a maelstrom of ashes, vampire-like, to the four winds. Georgia was as brutally hot and intensely humid as we remembered.

We had been lucky enough to have a private pool in the backyards of the two houses we had owned in the USA and we really wanted one here. I honestly just don't understand how you can live a meaningful life in the Deep South without a pool. People didn't even live here at all until the advent of air conditioning. In the years since 1950 when the A/C became available to most modern homes, the populations of the sunbelt states (Texas, Florida, Georgia, Arizona, Southern California, and New Mexico) suddenly increased by over one hundred million, lured south by the cooling purr of air conditioning. Fly over the northeastern states and you will see pool after pool glittering azure blue heat relief in backyards that are fifty percent of the time covered in snow. In Georgia very few.

We called a few pool companies but nobody was interested in building in Alpharetta. The reason being, that the good folks at City Hall had long since decided that the expensive improvement of an individual's home, to the benefit of all other residents within its city limits was an aberration to be frowned upon. Permits were required for most things, and as they related to pool building, everything. Setbacks, covenants, easements, zoning, trees, buffers, erosion, and sedimentation control barriers, the city document that *describes* the permitting procedure alone, runs to thirty-four pages. In neighboring cities, there are either none or extremely lax and flexible requirements for permitting and that's where the pool builders obviously prefer to ply their trade.

Cost is the other factor. If you have a specimen tree – you are shaking your head but if you are sitting reading this in an American subdivision, believe me, you do, the removal of that tree (or trees) requires a permit application, a meeting with the city arborist and removal by a tree surgeon. A single big tree can cost a thousand dollars and weeks of bureaucracy to cut down. Even a pine tree, which grows like a gargantuan weed anywhere and everywhere in Georgia, is a specimen tree if its trunk is more than thirty inches in diameter. One of the oddest requirements is that if you remove a tree you might have to replace it with a tree of similar standing. We love trees, particularly hardwoods, but where precisely should I do that for Christ's sake? Most of us don't own surplus land in which to replace a single tree never mind three or four. It was one of the reasons I wanted the damn thing out of my yard in the first place.

With the names in the directory of pool building companies almost exhausted, we had only one name remaining at the very bottom of the list, let's call him Todd. It was the guy who had built our last pool and we had sworn blood oaths, naked at midnight, dancing around the headless corpses of freshly slain chickens to not ever use him again.

Let's set one thing straight. The pool that Todd had built was phenomenal, we loved the end result and used it every day. In the end. It was the journey he took us all on to get to that end state that had left us with nervous ticks and a mild form of PTSD or pool traumatic stress disorder. And...in total fairness to the guy, our previous pool builder had been even worse. Todd operated from a level of cockiness that would have humbled a contestant on The Apprentice and casually spoke with a level of vulgarity that would have made a whore blush.

On that first pool adventure with Todd, we immediately ran into problems with permits on the build and Todd blamed everybody but he and his crew. One night I was out at dinner with some customers and Paula called. The pool, just a big dirty mud-filled hole at that point in its construction, was going to overflow and flood the house. We had been plagued by heavy rain from the very first moment the digger first broke ground, and this night the rain had been tropically torrential. I rushed home to find the orange, filthy mixture of clay mud, and rainwater just about to break over the edge of the construction. The pool had slowly filled and the small pump Todd had left on site had failed.

I quickly stripped out of my suit jacket and trousers. In a scene redolent of the end bit in Poltergeist, in my bare feet and underpants, I jumped into the muddy, water-filled pool, and with my nose inches from the surface of the murky cesspit, arms stretched, I felt around the bottom to finally locate and pull the pump out of the water. It had clogged with the detritus of the storm; the mud had plastered leaves solidly across the intake of the filter. I washed it clean and ran the drain line out to the street. With the pump re-started we managed to finally, slowly, win the battle against the rain and lower the water level.

The concrete gutters in the street from our house down the hill to the main storm drain were permanently stained a deep and dirty russet brown from that day forward. Somebody should really petition the city about having a permit set up so this sort of thing doesn't happen again.

We were reluctantly resigned to having to work with Todd once more and so we met with him the very next day. He immediately charmed us by asking how Adam was doing. Several years had passed but he remembered that Adam had been going through a tough patch while he was on site building the pool. It was sweet of him to remember that.

He explained that in the intervening years and since our absence, Alpharetta had gotten even worse about building regulations. He didn't say he didn't want to build the pool, but he clearly used language that suggested the difficulty Alpharetta would put him through would be plentifully reflected in the price to us. We parted on good terms. We would work on removing some trees, put up a fence around the property line, and get a land survey completed. After that, we could talk again and agree on a contract price.

Here is an interesting thing we had come to realize on our return to the USA. In their individual pockets of isolation, the UK had blamed Brexit and Boris Johnson in reasonably equal measures for sky-rocketing inflation, labor surplus, shortages of goods and the increase in prices they accrued. In the United States, the population blamed Biden or Trump, depending on your political affiliation.

The truth is that COVID had created a truly global situation, one where first the stock markets crashed, unemployment rose, the entire tourism industry collapsed and oil prices rose uncontrollably. Then, of course, just as recovery looked to be something the world could achieve, Russia invaded Ukraine. The world was feeling the impacts of the pandemic, not just in the city of Why, Arizona, or Whynot in North Carolina, not only in Dull in Scotland or the town of Kill in Ireland; the pandemic affected the entire global alphabetti spaghetti of cities, from Abidjan on the Ivory Coast to Zibo in China, every town and city across our entire planet.

You can hardly blame Boris and Donald for that. I do obviously, and you probably should too, but it's hardly fair when you really think about it...

That's when we discovered the price of everything in the US had risen exponentially, especially timber, and we had quite the fence to build.

LUMBERJACKS & CRIPS

With the water heater replaced with an expensive tankless boiler, we moved on to the bathroom renovations. We contracted Ernesto, a local tiler and general contractor who was well-regarded and strongly recommended by friends in the neighborhood. Originally from Mexico, he spoke excellent English but charmingly ended each sentence with the Spanish word for 'but' —*pero...* delivered with a shoulder shrug that spoke of a lack of certainty in all matters.

"I will definitely start the job tomorrow morning at 9 am promptly...pero..."

"I measured everything; I have everything I need to finish the job...pero..."

"I have made sure that the sealant around the shower is extra strong so it will never leak into the kitchen ceiling and ruin your house...pero..."

He subcontracted some of the more menial plumbing tasks to a Brazilian husband and wife duo called Maria and José. They were lovely but spoke not a single word of English. Paula and I spoke only a smattering of Spanish. Spanish and Portuguese share a lexical similarity of around 90%, but even so, many of the words have different pronunciations and syntax which brought a small thrill to each conversation. The two languages are surprisingly similar and yet dissimilar at the same time.

"Onde está a torneira?" asked José.

"Que?" I know he is asking where something is but I have no idea whatsoever what a torneira might be.

José mimes a tap being turned off. My lessons on Duolingo never included plumbing terms but given he is about to start some plumbing work; I think it's safe to assume that he means stopcock. Stopcock is another word far beyond my foreign language skills. I do know the word for tap though.

"el grifo de agua?"

"Sim, sim, a agua." He is animated here, smiling, I feel we are close to agreement.

"en el garaje."

"na garage?"

I am pretty sure, even though we are using differently sounding words that they share sufficient consonants and vowels to have a common ancestor, and we are both referencing the large space we keep the cars in, so I take him downstairs, walk over to where the gas and water pipes enter the building, and point at the stopcock.

"Allá. Ahí está el grifo." I say, hoping that I have remembered the correct Spanish for 'there' as in a thing quite close to me. The Spanish have three words for 'there'. One for things that are quite close, one for things over there, the other side of the room perhaps, and one for things that are way yonder, across town or in a different state.

"Sim, sim, a torneira! Obrigado."

He is still smiling and at last, I recognize the only Portuguese word I know, the one for thank you. Inordinately pleased with myself, we part company, proud that in a single day, I had effectively doubled my Portuguese vocabulary. Now I just need to wait, patiently, for the next opportunity to use stopcock and thank you, again, in a single sentence.

The bathroom was finally finished and was a gleaming jewel of a space in which to shower and bathe, a complete transformation from the gloomy, mildewed, and crack-tiled space it had once been. Unfortunately, José didn't seem to know his *esquerda* from his *certa*, or perhaps it was his *quente* from his *resfriado*. Whichever it was, when we ran a bath to luxuriate in our brand-new bathroom, hot water came out of the cold tap and cold water from the hot.

With the bathroom situation concluded we moved onto the yard. Paula contracted a local fencing company and with tree permits finally in place we also placed an order with a tree removal company. They all turned up together and mayhem ensued.

The pines we needed to remove were spectacular examples. Three of them towered over ninety feet into the air, creating a thick canopy through which almost no light penetrated to reach the barren earth beneath. With climbing irons strapped to his legs and a serious-looking chainsaw dangling from a rope on his harness, the lead lumberjack swiftly took to the skies. He scrambled up through the lower branches and appeared in his fluorescent safety jacket and orange helmet dizzyingly high in the canopy. Ropes were thrown and secured by the crew on the ground and with the rasp of the chainsaw the first heavy limb crashed through the foliage to land with a house-shaking WHUMP on the ground.

In next to no time all of the limbs were down and the ground crew dragged and pulled them toward the bobcat to be put through the woodchipper. Now only the trunk remained. It tapered from its massive girth at ground level to only a few feet around where we could still see the lumberjack, breathing hard and rocking gently as the remains of the tree swayed gently in the wind from the south.

Now only the hard work remained. The lumberjack lowered himself, and in six feet sections, ideal for later lumbering, sawed through the massive sections of trunk. The chainsaw howled and bark and chippings flew, thick through the air. There was a moment of serenity as the chainsaw completed its work and peace fell over the scene. Then the movement as the trunk section slowly freed itself from the remainder of its trunk and gravity pulled it in a serene arc toward the ground. It seemed to float, its mass hidden by the grace of its fall, interrupted only by the crash of window-rattling concussion as it hit and splintered onto the floor at its base.

One by one the crew dropped the sections of the trunk to the ground where they were taken by the bobcat to be stacked by the roadside for later collection.

In only an hour or so the trees were down, the yard cleared and the crew sat in the shade, soaked in sweat, wood chippings, and sawdust in their beards and hair, sharing jokes and swilling ice cold mountain dew. They were friendly efficient and pleasant.

The gang who turned up to build the fence was quite a different story. On our first contact with the fencing company, we met with a fresh-faced young, middle-class sales chap dressed in khaki slacks and those loafers Americans insist on wearing with the little tassels on the top. He walked the yard, took measurements and, with a broad and innocently reassuring smile, promised a quote by the end of the day.

By contrast, the crew who turned up to build the fence seemed to be on the run from a San Quentin State prison. I couldn't tell if they were Avenues, Crips, or Bloods but they acted more like an organized drugs cartel than folks familiar with carpentry. They refused to speak, and for a large portion of the day, they sat sulkily around on our lawn, talking and smoking, staring dead-eyed at us if we dared to venture to walk across our property while they were doing so. Despite their extended breaks and surly attitude, the fence only took a few days to complete.

When the head of the drugs cartel took some time away from his main day job to pretend that he was a fence builder, and finally ask me for payment, I insisted on walking the property line to make sure we were happy with the quality of the panels and doors they had erected. He narrowed his eyes and gave me a look like I was part of the Aryan Brotherhood and he was about to exact revenge for the repression of his people. It was like being in a bloodthirsty version of West Side Story — and I hate bloody musicals. We were ecstatic to have them off the property.

We got the site survey results the next day and we called Todd the pool guy to come back around to talk money and timings for the build of the new pool.

Disappointments

The bathroom was completed, the garden prepared and ready, and the patio built. All we needed now was the pool. In the sweltering heat, we measured it out with sticks and balls of gardening twine, debating where to have it and how large it should be. Todd had sent us some preliminary pricing which provided four different options, with prices varying by volume of both the pool itself and the concrete deck that would surround it.

Todd popped around to give us the bad news. The pricing he had given us was essentially garbage. Materials were in short supply and costs had rocketed, but the biggest problem, by far, was the city. Alpharetta had tightened their requirements on pool construction even more. The permitting application process was long and expensive and while Todd made reassuring noises about, maybe, perhaps, being able to start construction this year, it was clear that he had more than sufficient work in Canton, Woodstock, Forsyth, and Cobb to keep him busy. Anywhere in fact where pool construction was seen as a normal practice, indeed one that added significant value to a home and hence tax dollars to the city in which the home resided. He just didn't want the business. Too much hassle, too many hoops to jump through for the work it would bring him. We understood and shook hands goodbye in good faith.

It was a real blow. I am in no delusion as to how that sounds by the way. It is perhaps the definition of what constitutes a first-world problem. But it was really, really important to us. It was part of the deal I had made to Paula when we first moved to the USA fifteen years ago, part of the contract. If you move to somewhere hot, you get a pool to chill in.

Now we didn't know what to do. We spent some time tidying the garden. I built some raised beds for Paula to plant her herbs, tomatoes, and peppers, and one long weekend we decided to de-hydrate ourselves and nearly die by raking the chippings from the removed trees and planting grass seed on the barren mound of soil that we had created.

The grass seed, to our surprise, germinated and I spent hours, morning and night watering it. It worked so well that we planted seeds across much of the rest of the garden. It grew at an alarming rate and the garden suddenly became an oasis. Perhaps we could do without a pool? Just create a beautiful yard, fill it with grass and colorful shrubs, build some shade, and just enjoy the yard as it would become. And then, pretty much overnight all the grass just withered and died and nothing I did could stop its demise.

It was all very dispiriting. What's more, the cost of life back in the USA was crippling us. Paula had restarted her dog walking/sitting business and was doing a great trade in the neighborhood. My dream of funding a luxury lifestyle as an indie writer was not working out quite as well as I had expected though. The costs for house and car insurance were insane, fresh food was ridiculous and health insurance was a complete nightmare. It turned out that life in the USA was very different when you were pulling a salary from working for a large corporation, and quite the different thing when you were self-employed or semi-retired.

The housing market was incredibly buoyant and we started to think about treating this entire episode as a house flip. We had lots of fun dinners out with Adam but the hard truth is that he had his own life here, lots of friends and stuff to do without us. Ben was still in Japan and not in touch very often.

The situation with health care worried me, backed up by a trip to a doctor's office for something trivial. I joked as I handed over my health insurance card that we had terrible health coverage. The nurse took the card, glanced at it, and handed it back with a shake of her head and a, "You surely do honey, you surely do."

America is a wonderful, infuriating, admirable melting pot of anachronisms and contradictions. Its gun laws are a hot mess and unlikely to be changed anytime soon but its healthcare system is amongst the worst of the developed nations of the Economic Co-operation and Development (OECD). The US spends over 16% of its total GDP on healthcare. For reference, most of the thirty-eight members of the OECD spend around 10% of GDP on healthcare. I guess that anomaly would be fine if the healthcare that its citizens received was commensurate with the quality of life they received. But it isn't. Far from it. It's a nation where 62% of all bankruptcies of individuals are caused by the costs of healthcare. The USA was ranked 21st across the world by the SDG for the quality of healthcare provided. By comparison, the UK ranked 5th and Sweden 3rd. The USA's average life expectancy was lower and its infant mortality rate higher. It has become a country where it is cheaper to risk bleeding out in an Uber than to call an ambulance, and where health insurance views your eyeballs and teeth as optional extras.

The only way to remain in the US was for me to go back to work. Find a job back in corporate America and resume my old life flying coast to coast all week, spending days away in hotel rooms. It wasn't something I contemplated for long. As crazy as it sounds, after only a few months we decided to sell the house and return to the United Kingdom.

BUT WHERE?

We spoke to our realtor about the timing for putting the almost completely remodeled house back on the market. It was Summertime and if we acted quickly, we could catch the tail-end of the market was his advice. Prices were rising steeply and inventory remained low. We debated remaining in the house until Spring but were uncertain if the house price boom would remain in place (it would increase exponentially) and were also concerned if COVID cases would rise and impose more travel restrictions (they wouldn't). Hindsight is a real bitch.

We were also concerned about getting the dogs back to the UK. Many airlines had used the COVID crisis to distance themselves from the side operations they had long been forced by public opinion to tolerate. Pet transportation was one of them. It was always a terrible business for them to be in. A high-risk and low-margin enterprise, moving somebody's beloved family pet internationally, in a pressurized hold and in unpredictable temperatures at both departure and arrival airports, was just full of risk for the animals and the threat of litigation from the owners if something went wrong. Many had simply refused to carry on offering the service or imposed weight and size restrictions that would impact our ability to use them.

We also needed to find a place in the UK to live when we sold up in the USA, so we started to search around the town of Somerton, the same village that we had left only a few months ago. The village of Somerton is small. Founded in the 14th century it flirted with the title of county town of the county that was named for it. It is possible it was even the capital of ancient Wessex at one point. Still, it hasn't grown much since then. It is home to around five thousand residents, a small supermarket, a butcher's shop, four pubs, one fish and chip shop, and a Chinese takeaway. We like it a lot. It has a small village charm with enough stuff going on that you only have to go to nearby Yeovil for a "big shop", busier distractions like the cinema, and, every now and again, to have your pockets emptied at knifepoint.

Yeovil was mentioned in the Domesday Book and was once world-famous for its 19th-century leather glove industry. Now the locals call it *Yeo-vile* and it sadly has become the second most dangerous medium-sized town in Somerset, beaten only by nearby Bridgewater, which, if you believe the crime statistics, is even stabbier.

Yeovil measures second due to the 118 crimes that are reported to the police per 1,000 people. Pretty high when you consider Atlanta had only 45 reported crimes per 1,000 people in the same year. Of course, with all things American, you need to factor in that 158 people were murdered in Atlanta in 2021, and many of those homicides were associated with death by a gun. Nobody was actually killed in Yeovil. Overall, Somerset's County-wide crime rate is ridiculously low, it's a very safe place to live.

The problem for us was that there is never much for sale in the town of Somerton itself. There was a slew of new homes on the outskirts, being built by a company called Bloor Homes, and opposite where we used to rent on West Street an independent developer was building six new homes, three arranged in a terrace and three detached homes.

The Bloor homes were the standard cookie-cutter box homes of the modern housing estate, the style and build quality of which can be seen across the UK. There were a couple of floor plans we liked so we reached out to the sales team by email to get a better idea of pricing and, given they were still under construction, an estimate of when they would be available. That's when we found out that Bloor has an extremely bizarre purchasing policy which in fairness to them, they are very open about. If you decide to purchase a property, you get twenty-eight days to complete the sale. No arguments or discussions. They want all of your money in their bank account within those twenty-eight days. Bear in mind that the house might not yet be under construction and could take three to six months to complete.

Our other option was one of the three terrace homes being marketed by an estate agent in Somerton. The developer was building three terraced homes and three detached properties on the site of an old and abandoned garage and petrol station. The developer had creatively claimed that rather than having been a gas station forecourt, the site had been a former coach building yard and charmingly, imaginatively, and somewhat deceitfully called the development The Old Coachworks. Each of the homes was named after an 18th-century horse-drawn coach, Gig Cottage, Hackney Cottage, Brougham House, Landau House, Phaeton House, and Surrey House, you know, the one with the fringe on the top.

Both builders sent us floor plans and pricing and we spent the next few days poring over plans and comparing prices and specifications.

The two options posed different conundrums for us. The Bloor homes were detached, large, and modern. They presented traditional floorplans, a kitchen diner with a separate living room and four bedrooms upstairs, one ensuite, and a family bathroom shared by the other three. They presented the opposite of individuality, designed to leech any character and country charm from their uniform brick facades and compartmentalized and identically planted front gardens. Nonetheless, they looked to be well built, all had detached garages and small but almost adequate parcels of grass in the back gardens for the dogs to slowly scorch brown. The downsides were that they were not actually in the village and we would be living on an estate.

The terraced houses, on the other hand, were located close to the center of the village. But the floorplans looked tight even as they offered something a little more unique. The three terraces were similar but not quite the same. They all had one kitchen diner that led straight into a living space with tri-fold doors at the rear that led onto a small garden. Depending on the plan they had either two or three bedrooms on the next floor with a family bathroom, and on the top floor a master bedroom with En-suite.

Being who we had become, we called the sales teams of both developments from America and tried to buy one of the houses sight unseen over the phone. We figured both houses were in the village we liked and it didn't need to be our forever home. It would be bricks and mortar back in the UK, and if we decided to move in a year or so we probably wouldn't lose money.

You could buy a house over the phone with ease in America given a sufficiently rosy credit rating (God bless her beating black capitalist heart), but not in Europe. An American salesperson would have cashed your check and charged that card as soon as you uttered the phrase, "I deserve it. I'll just take the one in blue right now."

In England, you could almost hear the eyebrows of suspicion being raised on the other end of the line. Were we international money launderers? A drugs cartel with some sinister, albeit creative and illegal use for a small residential property in rural Somerset?

Regardless, the salespeople of both properties refused us point blank. We would need to view the properties, in person, before they would even consider an offer. This seemed somewhat onerous in the days of COVID and Zoom meetings, but both parties were veritable brick walls of denial. First, we had to prove we had funds and I spent a few hours on the phone back to the UK with finance managers and sales managers, sending bank statements and other financial documents back and forth. Finally, we had two appointments scheduled. One to view the estate house on the Bloor Homes development and one to view the terrace homes in the center of Somerton.

So, a week or so later I found myself sitting in a medical cubicle in a Walgreens in Canton waiting for the results of my PCR COVID test, the one I would need to be negative so that I could catch my flight back to the UK the next day, to view two potential homes for us. We had decided that I would travel solo. It would be easier and cheaper for Paula to remain in the UK to look after the dogs. The test itself had proved a challenge to book. The US prided itself on the availability of testing, but the number of centers that had the facilities available to provide instant results were startlingly scarce. I had to drive forty miles to my appointment.

BLOOR

This would be a whistlestop, jet-lagging challenge of a week. My plan was to keep the trip as short as possible. Fly out Sunday night, meet with Bloor Homes and the estate agency representing the Coachworks development, and fly back into Atlanta on Thursday. I would have done it even quicker if I could, but I would need time for the PCR test I would need to take on arrival in the UK to be processed so that I could travel back home.

Delta had abandoned the useless COVID testing app, so I just printed all of the paperwork for the test results along with my passenger locator forms needed for entry back into the UK. The passenger locator forms were a bit of a rip-off and, judging by the number of American travelers queuing up at the gate in the international terminal on Sunday evening, a fairly well-kept international secret. Almost nobody had one, and the problem for the gate agents who were collecting paperwork was that the forms also carried the requirement to have listed on them an official booking number for the two COVID tests that needed to have been pre-booked and pre-paid for. One test was needed on day two of arrival and another needed five days after arrival. Without the booking numbers, the forms were useless.

It wasn't clear to me how the problems for the intended travelers were going to be resolved, I rather suspected it wasn't and that the likelihood of them flying that night was slim. When I boarded, the flight was certainly less than half capacity.

I landed at Heathrow and, bleary-eyed and yawning widely, I used my British passport to pass through the uncrowded and automated immigration desk. I had all my important paperwork in hand, ready to surrender to the border agents but there was absolutely nobody in the arrivals hall to check either vaccination status or the traveler location forms I had carefully printed off.

I had booked a private car which was thankfully waiting for me. The day was bright and warm and the driver, whose name was Michael, was extremely chatty, but the banter kept me awake and we covered the miles quickly. *Really* quickly. I had forgotten how fast the British drive. Michaels's surname could have been Schumacher. With tires screeching and gravel flying at other passengers waiting for a taxi, we hurtled out of Heathrow and tore around the M25 like a rider on the wall of death. I had my face pressed up against the passenger door window as we exited the roundabout onto the A303, and with Stonehenge a blur in his mirrors, Michael pulled up with a squeal of tires outside the Boot's chemists in Glastonbury only a little more than an hour later. I had assumed we would travel within, or at least close to, the posted speed limits of the roads we traveled, so I found myself almost an hour early for the first of my COVID tests.

Of course, the brevity of my visit meant that even though I had had to pay for the day five test, by the time that came due I would already be back in America. Well, I would be back in America if I passed this first test. I had no contingency plan in place if I were to test positive, and I wouldn't get the results until close to the time I needed to catch the flight home.

I had a strong cup of coffee seated in a delightful café on the High Street and watched the genuine weirdness of an early morning in the small town of Glastonbury come to life. The Boots chemist was right across the road so, somewhat caffeinated and awake, I walked across and asked if they could bring my test forward by an hour. The shop was small and empty and the clinician seemed happy for something to do.

The nasal swabs we had done in the US were gentle, nasal tickling experiences of the outer nostrils. Not so in the UK. The nurse, I graciously allow that title, clamped a gloved hand across my forehead and, so secured against escape, with a long and pokey swab in the other she explored the periphery of my brain stem with such pep and vigor that I smelt colors for a day or more.

England was still coming out of lockdown and most of the people in the stores and even walking around outside wore masks. With a tissue dabbing my sensitive nose holes, I ambled across to where a taxi sat idling in a cloud of diesel fumes. I slipped my mask on as I approached.

"Can you take me to Somerton please?"

The driver was a normal-looking middle-aged guy, with grey hair and brown spectacles. He wore taupe slacks and a cardigan. My heart sank, he looked just like the sort who might read the Mail on Sunday or watch Fox News and couldn't wait to share his ideologies with a captive passenger. The sort who may carry some sketchy right-wing beliefs about immigrants and the place of gays and women in the workplace that most would find cringy to hear, but to my surprise, as are most things in Glastonbury, he was a delight.

"Sure, my lovely. And you don't need to wear that mask in the car if you don't want to."

I noticed for the first time that he didn't have one.

"You all stopped wearing them then?"

"We never wore them around here. Not once. Utter bunkum, the whole thing."

Ok, so perhaps there was the sniff of the conspiracy theorist about him, but he was very friendly and completely accepting of the strange folks who wandered through the town he called home. On the short journey, he told me about a chap who turned up in town, one day, entirely out of the blue. He was dressed as a Roman Centurion, the full regalia, real steel armor, a plumed helmet, sword, ankle boots, the whole thing. He would march around town, silent and aloof, never made a single friend and never appeared out of his uniform, and then two years later disappeared without a trace. Nobody knew who he was or why he did what he did. How wonderful is that? It sums up Glastonbury perfectly.

The taxi dropped me outside the AirBnB in which I would be stopping. I dropped my backpack off and walked through the village. I grabbed a bacon sandwich and a cold bottle of orange juice from Burns the Bread, had a pee in the public toilets behind the library, and sweating in the unseasonable heat of the day, I walked across town to meet with the sales team at Bloor homes and to view the build they had insisted I travel 4000 miles, during a pandemic, to see.

It was quite a hike in the heat. I had only brought jeans with me, dressing for an English summer of rain showers and chilly winds. I stopped for a few minutes to sit panting on a bench that overlooked the fisheries and the levels that lay spread out below me like some vast emerald baize-covered snooker table. The countryside here, which sits between the rolling hills, is in reality a vast coastal plain that has been drained since the days of the Domesday Book. Without the active draining and pumping, these lush fields would flood again, as most of the flat lands lie at, or slightly below, sea level. In the Middle Ages, the nearby monasteries of Glastonbury, Athelney, and Muchelney were responsible for much of the drainage.

In those days, in winter, the fields would be left to flood, bringing rich sediments back to the land. Somerset is actually named for 'the land of the summer people' as before the Dutch, bless them, solved all of the drainage problems in the 17th century, the fertile grazing pastures of the Levels were only habitable in the drier months. On a quiet day, you can still hear the rhythmic thump, thump, thump of the pumping stations.

The walk to the Bloor Homes development took me past the edge of the industrial estate and I had a sinking feeling straight away as I walked onto the site. The houses on the edge of the development were already occupied. I peered into one of the front gardens. The lawn was bare and full of dandelions and thistles, children's toys lying forsaken amongst the piles of dog shit. The house was brand new but already looked scruffy and uncared for. As I walked past, the door opened and a young woman in crumpled pajamas and pink fluffy slippers stepped out and caught me peeking into her yard. I never had much of a poker face and I guess she could read my snooty expression of undeserved judgment. She had a cigarette in one hand and fixed me with a gaze that screamed "What the fuck are you looking at." She made a good point. I chided myself silently for being an opinionated baldy bastard and gave her a little wave of apology as I hurried on.

Rows of purposefully dissimilar homes, some finished and occupied set amidst a busy building site. I found the sales office and, checking that I was on time, pressed the buzzer on the door of the show house to gain entry.

A young woman opened the door and I explained who I was. It was no understatement to say my mind was entirely boggled when she explained that the sales manager and finance manager, the very people I had made all of the arrangements with to visit, were not in fact there. Not only were *they* absent but the plot that we wanted to buy, wasn't available to view due to construction work being done close to it. I sat dumbfounded in a chair, enjoying the air-conditioning, while she pointlessly banged on about dates for availability and upgrade options. She offered to show me a house that was nothing like the floor plan we wanted to buy, and with nothing else to do for the day, I followed her around as she tried in vain to describe how our floor plan would be different.

"Ignore the bedroom we are standing in, yours will be much bigger with an En-suite...and an extra window...and on a different floor actually. Nothing like this in fact...but it will be lovely."

It was an outrageous level of disrespect for me, my time, and the enormous cost and stress they had put me through. There was no point in venting to the young woman they had left to deliver the bad news, but Bloor Homes was now permanently bereft of a buyer.

It was a long walk back into town which further cemented the decision for me. Even if the assholes had let me view the house, I didn't want to live on an estate, and living so far from the village center defeated the point of being here. I wanted to be able to walk to the butcher's shop to get ham for lunch, and to the convenience store to get a bottle of wine, and every now and again saunter into town to get a fancy dinner at the White Hart.

I thought about getting a table there now and enjoying a pint with dinner, but I just couldn't face sitting in there on my own, so I grabbed a bottle of wine, a scotch egg, and a pack of pre-made sandwiches (all-day breakfast I think) and headed to my lonely room in the Airbnb. I chatted with Paula on WhatsApp and explained the situation with Bloor and she immediately began to craft a strongly worded email to them. I scattered crumbs across the bed and scratched my sore nostrils while I admired the lilac-painted bedroom. Hmmm, that color smells of lavender I thought as I wrinkled my nose. Within ten minutes I was fast asleep.

COACHWORKS

I woke up early and showered. Feeling immensely better, I changed clothes and headed out. I had a meeting with the estate agent who was selling the Coachworks properties and she was bringing Jim, who was the owner and developer. He had driven down from London to meet with me, something, which after yesterday's rude disappointments, I was somewhat skeptical about happening.

When I set off on my short walk the sun had been belting down on my bald head. Ten minutes later, as I was standing on the edge of the building site the clouds had rolled in, the skies darkened and the heavens had opened. There was nobody there waiting for me and with nowhere to shelter I was quickly drenched. I had a quick nosy around the building site. Two of the larger detached homes were nearing completion but the rest were just foundations, two courses of breeze block and mud.

I began to wonder, as I splashed around in sodden socks and squeaky shoes, what had possessed me to come all this way, to not see anything at Bloor and deflatingly stare at muddy bricks here. I was awakened from my reverie by a cheery voice. It was the estate agent, Kerry, walking down the access road that would one day become Coachworks Mews, followed close behind by Jim.

Jim was a breath of fresh air and we hit it off immediately. He was a little younger than me and his enthusiasm was totally infectious. He was genuinely proud of what he was building. He showed me the tri-fold doors on one of the detached properties and pointed out the quality of the insulation and the type of Indian stone being used for the patios. I called Paula and using WhatApp video showed her the floor layouts. There wasn't much to see, knee-high breeze blocks outlined where the main structural walls would be, but even the strongest of imaginations would struggle to make a home out of the mud, puddles, and piles of cement.

It couldn't be denied that they were small though. From where we stood at the rear of the house, I could see people walking past on West Street where the front door might one day be, we were so close we could easily converse and, if we all leaned in a bit, could almost shake hands.

Still, it was a helpful visualization. We thought we had favored the end terrace, but on seeing how the access from the rear worked, how the middle terrace was larger with an extra bedroom, and being the only one with a detached garage on the development we decided on plot two.

I shook Jim's hand; told him we wanted that one, and then asked Kerry when they would be ready for us to move in. It was the middle of August already and Kerry suggested the end of November. Jim gave me a knowing wink behind Kerry's back and whispered that they would be completed and ready for habitation long, long before that.

The next day I had the morning to myself, still anxiously waiting for my COVID test results to come through. I walked across the fields

where we had walked the dogs almost every day. The fields were tall
with corn that swayed and rustled in that disconcerting manner that
they always manage to convey in films about alien abduction and
disturbed locals with chainsaws. I turned at the top of the hill and
looked back down on the village. It was lovely, rustic, and ancient to an
extreme, the bell tower of St Michael & All Angels a blue stone finger
against the sheep-scattered emerald backdrop of Hurcot Hill.

The house we...I...had chosen, was a concern. I was uncomfortable
with making such a decision without Paula, but with nothing else for
sale in Somerton and no time or ability to look elsewhere there was
really no other choice. It would just have to work itself out over time.
Just as I turned to walk back towards the village to get some lunch
my phone pinged. I opened the email from Boots with shaking hands.
The test was negative. I could travel home tomorrow.

In the afternoon Michael Schumacher picked me up, and white
knuckle whisked me back to Heathrow where I arrived an hour before
check-in opened. I stopped overnight in the same windowless airport
hotel we had stopped at six months ago, eating pre-packaged sandwiches, drinking wine, and watching repeats of One Foot in the Grave
on the tiny TV.

Heathrow in the morning was funereal, somber, and quiet. It was
difficult to imagine it busy and crowded ever again. I grabbed a bottle
of water and yet another all-day breakfast sandwich for the flight and
sat, sweating slightly, in the baleful glare of sunshine through the not
quite tinted enough floor-to-ceiling windows, passing time until my
flight was called, watching airplanes taxiing to and from gates and
wondering where they were all going.

The flight home was reassuringly uneventful. I caught an Uber
outside the international terminal to begin what turned out to be the
surprisingly most exciting part of the entire journey. My young black

male driver apologized as he was running low on gas and needed to stop. We exited Hartsfield Jackson and pulled into a seedy-looking gas station and combined Braids & Beauty store in College Park. Fully fueled, rather than join the highway, to my surprise he took the back-streets through East Point, Oakland City, and Adair Park, some of the most notoriously dangerous neighborhoods in Atlanta.

The houses there are mostly single-story ranch houses, many aban-doned and boarded. Unlike the swanky subdivisions of North At-lanta, businesses are interspersed amongst the homes, breakers yards, a towing and impound yard, and a tire and rims store. We crossed rail tracks and cruised slowly past the Baptist Church of True Deliverance on Capitol View, Oakland City.

Oakland City is a very different place from where we were extremely privileged to work and spend our leisure time. Where we lived, in Alpharetta, violent crime is measured at a tiny rate of 0.0242 per 100K people and property crime is at 0.1068 per 100K people. Compare that to the area I was being driven through now, where the violent crime rate is currently measured at 1246 per 100K people, and its property crime rate is 3027 per 100K people.

The difference comes down to one city, Alpharetta, where crime, to any real extent, simply does not exist, to another where it is a daily circumstance of a life born poor.

83% of Oakland City is populated by African Americans and their median household income is a paltry $27,270. By contrast, Alpharetta is 88% populated by either white or Asian people who enjoy a lifestyle where their households take home on average a lavish $153,808. Both cities enjoy comparable levels of education, and I'm certainly not qualified to comment on why the differences are so stark, certainly not in a little travel adventure book that's supposed to be a touch on the droll side, but available choices must surely play a part.

Oakland City and Alpharetta, and hundreds of others like them in the USA, are literally worlds apart but, in fact, separated by only tens of miles.

I played it as cool as any middle-aged white guy could, as we passed through row upon row of decrepit housing and gas station forecourts and grocery stores crowded with gangs of black, hard-staring young men, all looking in our direction as we cruised slowly by.

My phone buzzed quietly and when I glanced down, even the Uber App was worried about me. The message on the screen read "It looks like you are away from your expected route. Would you like us to call 911?"

I was starting to think this might end badly and seriously considered having Uber send the vehicle details and location to the police when we turned a corner and there stood the gleaming, silver-paneled roof of the Mercedes Benz stadium in downtown. At last, I knew where I was. My driver obviously hearing my sigh of relief, hissed through gritted teeth. He turned with a broad smile.

"Man...I bet you thought you was done for huh Bro?"

I laughed along with him, more in relief to be honest, and started to compose the post-ride survey.

"One star! Prick!"

ANOTHER FAREWELL

A week after my return from the UK we had our yard sale on a beautiful Saturday morning. Unlike the one we had in February, more than a year ago, this one was wildly successful. The usual early morning crush of Mexican workers spilled across the lawn to pillage the garden and power tools, and we quickly sold a host of tables, chairs, lamps, and rugs.

An odd Chinese lady arrived and bought a few items, some cutlery, and a free-standing lamp. She spoke very little English and would disappear to her car for several minutes and then reappear. She seemed interested in a really nice chrome leg and glass-topped dining table we had bought. It was a really good item and we wanted a few hundred dollars for it, less than half of what we had bought it for. She made a few crazy offers in her broken English and I kept insisting on the asking price. Paula could see me struggling with her and gave me a wink and a cheeky grin, happy that it was me having to negotiate with her.

Finally, the Chinese lady gave in and bought the table and then asked me to take it apart and put it in the boot of her car. I muttered a quiet "for fucks sake," to myself, but there were only two bolts on the pedestal that attached to two long iron rods that fed through the legs to secure the top, so I quickly flipped the whole thing upside down, undid the bolts and stripped the unit apart. The Chinese lady watched my every move intently as I did so. When it was disassembled, I took it, piece by piece, and placed it carefully on some rags in the boot of her brand-new silver Lexus, and off she drove.

Busy with other buyers I didn't notice the Lexus pull up twenty minutes later. Paula grabbed my elbow and squeezed to whisper, "She's back," in my ear. The Chinese lady had got home and realized she had no idea how to put the table back together. We were really busy with other buyers, but I suppressed a loud sigh and walked her slowly and diligently through the assembly process, pointing to each component as I did so. I even sketched the pieces out for her and the order in which they needed to be used on a piece of scrap paper and, nodding confirmation of her understanding, off she went again.

Thirty minutes later my heart sank to see her pull up to the curb once more. She looked pissed off and started miming that the table was broken and wobbly, or at least that's what I think she was saying. She asked me to follow her home to see what was wrong. I mean really, who does that for something purchased at a yard sale? And what utter dipshit idiot then agrees to drive to a complete stranger's house to help with a sold-as-seen item, purchased for half its true market value? Well, I did obviously.

Luckily, she only lived five minutes away, in a really salubrious neighborhood that brimmed with million-dollar homes. She pulled up the large curving drive and parked her Lexus in her three-car garage. I parked our car on the street and grabbed some tools, a wrench to tighten the nuts on the underside of the table, and a hammer in case somebody else was inside waiting to jump me. The house on the outside was HOA immaculate. Freshly washed paint and windows, a pretty garland on the shining front door. Perfectly tended flower beds, perfectly symmetrical Crepe Myrtles, and a lawn manicured to bowling green perfection.

The inside of the huge house was as rank as the floor in a Waffle House kitchen. Dirty clothes and used, crumpled underwear lay strewn across the stained carpet and stairs. Bowls of half-eaten cereal were discarded on the floor, one tipped half over, spilling milk carelessly onto a rug where two small grimy, and barely clothed children lay. They looked up, blank-eyed and disinterested as I walked by, stepping carefully through the upended toys and torn paper and cardboard that had just been thrown on the floor. Dust lay thick on all the kitchen surfaces and the sink was piled high with stained and dirty plates. Take-out boxes tumbled to the floor, fallen from the too-full bin in the corner, sending wafts of stale pizza and noodles through the too-warm space. I expected to see cockroaches but there was no sign of them, although it was just a matter of time before they took up residence and subsequent control of the house. The Chinese lady didn't seem to care what I thought about the state of the house, which was certainly for the best.

As I followed her through the house, I checked every room and every corner for a hidden accomplice who might leap out to abduct my saggy middle-aged white ass for a paltry profit on the white slave trade. But other than her and the seemingly catatonic children we appeared to be alone. I followed her into the kitchen and there was the glass-topped table. She grabbed the glass and shook it and sure enough, it wobbled on its chromium legs. She said something angrily in Chinese which I ignored, flipped the table upside down, and checked the bolts. They were both less than finger loose. I grabbed the wrench from my pocket and nipped them up nice and tight, flipped the table back on its pedestal, and gave it a good shake. Rock solid.

The Chinese lady looked at me, eyes wide, like I had suddenly appeared in a puff of white smoke wearing a black cape, a badly cut scene from a Harry Potter movie, and stared at my wrench like it was a wand purchased from Olivander's for the princely sum of seven Galleons. She made a surprisingly quick grab for it and I held it comically aloft, like keeping candy from a petulant toddler.

"Give it to me," she hissed as she danced and hopped on frustrated tiptoes before me.

I suddenly felt like Frodo, holding the ring of power out of the reach of poor Smeagol, transformed into the ugly, grasping Gollum by its mind-corrupting power.

"Mine!" I said, falling straight into the unexpected role she seemed to have cast for me. And then recovering my composure, "Jesus, lady, it's just a wrench," muttered as I backed up and walked briskly to the door to escape this house of sudden and unexpected suburban insanity.

Our house went on the market while the painters were still finishing the exterior. The market was booming, with many houses selling before they were even listed, often for significantly over the asking price. Our realtor got very excited and wanted to test the market with a seriously high price. We were less certain, hopeful, but less certain. The house was nice and we had spent a lot of money to modernize it, but it was still one of the smaller floor plans in the neighborhood, with a slightly strange, disjointed layout of bedrooms upstairs.

Over the next few days, we had a serious amount of foot traffic, and sat outside in the car with air conditioning blasting, while we watched family after family, and realtor after realtor march through the house. We dashed back inside between viewings to turn the lights back on, tidy up, and to have a pee. To everybody's surprise, we got no offers.

Of course, it finally sold and at not a terrible price, but certainly nowhere near where the market predicted it would. With a thirty-day close, we were lucky to know that a house in the neighborhood lay empty and the owner would be happy to consider a short-term lease. They had bought the house just before the pandemic had begun and had never lived in it permanently. With not much of our furniture left, we either sold or gave away what little remained and began moving the clothes, documents and increasingly despairing pups into the rental property.

With our focus on minimizing the number of possessions we owned, it was quite a surprise to return home one afternoon to find a large cardboard box propped up outside the garage. The box was four feet tall and travel-worn, plastered with import and export stamps and shipping labels, torn, removed, and replaced. It was addressed to me, so I carried the box inside and still scratching my head as to what it could be, I used a knife to cut the packing tape that secured it. Opening the last flap of cardboard was like opening the lid of the mysterious briefcase at the end of Pulp Fiction. A light filled the room, reflected from the gorgeous sensual curves of a beautiful Red Cedar Breedlove acoustic guitar with customized inlaid mother-of-pearl flowers on the bridge.

There was a note inside, handwritten by a dear friend. The guitar had been purchased well over a year ago, as a leaving present from my friends on the management team I had been a part of, back in the USA. I was still baffled by how it had just turned up at the house we were about to leave so I made some calls.

The guitar had quite the story to tell of its epic journey. It had begun its travels in Maryland USA where a friendly grey-bearded man in a pork pie hat made certain that it was carefully packaged in a new and sturdy cardboard box and placed the package into the competent and reassuringly expensive hands of UPS.

A long plane journey later found it in a sweltering customs office in Madrid, where it languished for quite a while under the painfully slow bureaucracy, expertly exercised by every Spanish official. Finally released from its enforced confinement, it traveled overland, across the Spanish steppes, on trains and trucks to arrive at the gates of a Spanish villa in the dusty hills outside Altea, only a week or two after we had departed its doors. Back on trains, trucks, and planes it slowly found its way, its box a little battered and bearing the stamps and insignia of prolonged travel, all the way back to the now puzzled man in a pork pie hat.

With a new address in his contacts, back to the UPS depot, he drove, and once more sent the guitar eastward, this time towards England. It arrived in Heathrow and the efficient customs operative dispatched it with minimal delay to an address in sleepy Somerset. It arrived three days after we had moved on once more, this time back to America.

Back in Heathrow, the guitar's battered packaging was taped and repaired, and a new consignment notice was taped to make sure it would arrive back in Maryland within the week. On an increasingly familiar doorstep, the guitar was signed for and the aggrieved wife of the increasingly baffled pork pie-wearing man was heard to shout "did you buy *another* bloody guitar?"

One more time the guitar's cardboard box was taped and repaired and a new delivery address was taped to the exterior which, graffitied as it was by the customs stamps of numerous international countries, was beginning to resemble the inside of 007's passport. And so it was that fifteen months later, finally, I took possession of my leaving present surprise, my precious little twangy Breedlove.

With our new house in the UK not being ready to move into until towards the end of November, we decided to live the romantic life of Romany gypsies for a few months, spend a week or so In Yorkshire, and then work our way down the length of the UK, visiting places we either hadn't been too for a long time, or better still places we had never visited. We would begin our journey in our hometown of Southport. We had a small support structure of friends there and obviously knew the town intimately. It was also only forty miles from Manchester airport, ideal for getting the dogs couriered to, without them having to suffer a long onward road journey.

The day of the closing was perfunctory. We drove to mid-town, signed the house over to the lovely young couple who had bought it, and drove back to our rental. Everything was finally organized. Flights had been a logistical challenge, but we had our flights booked and so did little Pi and Archie. The dogs had watched us pack and prepare their crates. Pi hid in the bedroom and Archie put his paw over his brown eyes and shook his fluffy head in quiet dismay.

Nobody was flying directly to Manchester. We all had to fly through Amsterdam, and the pups had it worse than us because due to flight availability, by the time they landed in Holland, they wouldn't have time to clear doggy customs and make their onward connection. We would all just have to meet up at the Airbnb Paula had booked in our old hometown of Southport the next day.

We started to, once more, say all of our goodbyes. We flew down to Fort Myers to spend the weekend with Alma our dear friend who had departed Atlanta only weeks before we arrived, to slowly burn herself golden brown in the endless sunshine. We had drinks around the neighborhood pool and farewell wings and ranch-covered fries.

In hindsight, the flights to Fort Myers were probably ill-timed. The airports were surprisingly busy and crowded with both masked and unmasked travelers. To enter England, we had to take and pass another PCR test and had booked into the same Walgreens in Canton I had used for my last UK trip. On the day of the test, I had a slight cough and felt a little feverish, nothing serious, but it raised the stakes to a level I could have done without, with our flights back to the UK booked for the very next day. Sat in the chair while the machine whirred and clicked through its test, I pondered the variables if mine came back positive. Paula would need to fly on her own to make sure somebody was in Southport to take receipt of the dogs. I would need to re-book everything and hang out in the rental until I once more tested negative. It was doable but would be a real hassle. So, I greeted the negative result with a huge sigh. I coughed with relief all the way home.

The next day we drove the car to CarMax and then to a cash machine to deposit the check, picked up a Subway, and finished packing our few bags. Most of our belongings had already been sent on ahead, to be stored once more in the garage of the ever-long-suffering Kaz and Steve. We would pick them up in a month or so when the house became ready to move into.

We filled our remaining evenings cramming more hot wings and juicy burgers down our throats. On our last night, we had dinner with Adam at Longhorn steakhouse.

Then the day of departure arrived. We had to leave for the airport before the dogs got picked up, so we left the travel cages and precious paperwork with Adam. He would remain at the rental house and wait for the courier. Our old friend and neighbor Bob pulled up in his truck and, suddenly, it was time to say goodbye once again.

We had done this way too often recently. I tried to choke back the tears as I hugged Adam a farewell in a voice croaky and raw with emotion. In the end, it was his fault, he hugged me so hard he squeezed the tears from my eyes. We laughed in manly discomfort and patted each other on the backs in the way that useless men do sometimes when overwhelmed with those pesky 'emotion' things. Paula was crying openly, which was the right thing to do, and I found that I just couldn't make myself look back, to see Adam standing alone once more, as we pulled out of the neighborhood to head to the airport.

SOUTHPORT

We had a beer in Terminal E at Atlanta airport. International flights normally leave from the new dedicated international terminal, but for some reason, we had been relegated to the crowded, older terminal for our Delta flight to Amsterdam. That evening, I flew out of Atlanta at age fifty-five and landed in Amsterdam on the morning of my fifty-sixth birthday.

The flight was busy and we landed on time. We had all of the paperwork printed off and safely stored in my backpack. Based on recent travel I suspected we wouldn't need it to get through immigration and join our connecting flight to Manchester. I was very wrong. We were hustled through the large terminal, from one side all across to the other, to queue at a check-in desk that was being used to process inbound travelers. Tall, beautiful, friendly, blond people were checking all paperwork, passports, vaccination status, and traveler locator forms. Each document was carefully studied and finally, each passport was stamped and a sticker placed on the back to let the next gate agent we were safe to board. Pleased with our little stickers, we were hustled all the way back across the terminal to find our gate.

We were pretty tired but took our assigned seats, squeezed between a couple of businessmen on the KLM flight, and lay back to enjoy the short hop across the English Channel and overland flight toward Manchester. When we took off, we were pleasantly surprised by the flight crew. They had realized that it was my birthday, a fact that I had certainly forgotten! They kindly moved us to better seats and brought me a lovely card signed by the crew and a small bottle of champagne. I was thrilled. I had painfully earned platinum medallion status on Delta over the course of sixteen years, had flown tens of thousands of miles with them, domestic and international, and they had never upgraded me or even recognized that I existed. On my first KLM flight, they gave me a bloody birthday party!

Nobody in the UK checked any paperwork, perhaps because KLM had taken the ownership, but we cleared customs, jumped in the taxi we had booked, and arrived completely shagged out in Southport. The Airbnb we had booked was a converted coaching house around the back of a large, detached property. It was clean and roomy with a comfortable lounge and kitchen and three bedrooms with a family bathroom. Now we just needed to await the arrival of Pi and Archie.

We paced around the property and Paula checked her phone constantly for updates. An hour or so later we got a call from the driver, he was just pulling up outside. We had sworn to the dogs, who I swear nodded in understanding as I told them, that we would never make them fly ever again. As a sign of good faith, when we unloaded them from the back of the van, we donated the expensive travel cages to the RSPCA and the driver took them away. The dogs had been treated well; they looked hot and stressed but were excited to see us, and after a cold drink of water and a sniff and a pee in the unfamiliar garden they cuddled up to us on the couch to join us in a well-earned and much-needed doze.

The next morning an old friend of mine from when we both worked at British Telecom pulled into the drive. We had asked Adrian to drive us to Manchester to pick up a green and white Mini Cooper S we had bought, sight unseen, over the phone from pictures on the internet.

Me and Adrian had been best friends since we met. I was a young telephone engineer who drove a little yellow Vauxhall Viva van with ladders on the top. Adrian was a mechanic in the BT workshop. I can't even remember how we became friends, but I guess we just hit it off. I got moved to Business Systems which meant I got to ditch my overalls and instead, wear black trousers and a tie. At the time I thought I was the mutt's spuds. I finally convinced Adrian to move out of the garage and join me on the team. We shared an entirely puerile shade of humor and had an absolute hoot of a time together. We weren't really supposed to be together half of the time, but this was in the glorious days before GPS tracking and electronic job sheets. We worked in the happy days when the engineers called a disinterested chap called Bob who sat in a control center somewhere in Preston. Me and Adrian would be sat drinking tea in a telephone exchange and would call in together, pool our jobs, knock them out together as quickly as we could, and then go for a drive in the country somewhere, enjoy a game of squash or have a cold pint by a canal.

One day we were sat together in the van, our jobs for the day done, hiding from the bosses, when I mentioned a British magazine called Viz. It's essentially an adult comic full of the most juvenile, rude and profane characters like Terry Fuckwit, The Fat Slags, and Buster Gonads, a young man who had such unfeasibly large testicles he had to lug them around in a wheelbarrow. My favorite character was a baker called Fru T. Bunn. He made gingerbread sex dolls for his own nefarious purposes. They were made out of gingerbread obviously, but also sported meringue breasts and a donut 'minge piece.' Adrian hadn't heard of the comic but, now massively intrigued, he made me drive immediately into town to buy a copy. We then parked up on a side street, two middle-aged men giggling like naughty schoolboys, tears streaming and stomachs aching. I know, I know, totally immature. Still the *size* of those testicles!

With Adrian's help, he drove us to pick up the Mini and I drove it back to Southport, parting ways with Adrian, but promising to meet up with him in town in a couple of hours for a pint.

An hour or so had passed since my last meal and I was starting to feel fractious, so we stopped for lunch on the way home at one of our favorite country pubs, The Plough at Lathom. On Sundays, they do a wonderful carvery. Paula and I, along with Ben and Adam, when they were kids, took my dad there on Christmas day the year Mum died. We couldn't face trying to emulate my Mum's Christmas dinner and thought a change of venue might keep all of those glorious happy memories at bay. Now I write it down, I see what a silly thing that was to attempt. Still, the lunch they served that day we picked up the Mini was as good as I remembered. It's one of those menus where everything looks at least as good as everything else, and you end up over-ordering, terrified in case you miss out on something.

With me fueled for at least another hour or so, we parked up the Mini back at the rental, checked on the dogs, and then walked into the town that we used to think of as our own, but which we hadn't visited in years. Growing up in the 1970's it had been an absolute idyll. Located on the Northwest coast, barely twenty miles north of Liverpool, the town began as a commune of fifty huts called *Otergimele,* as it was then listed in the Domesday Book. A primitive church was built on the location of what would become modern-day Churchtown.

I love how that happens in English, somebody builds a church and it becomes referred to as the town with the church—Churchtown. English is replete with such, occasionally abstract etymologies. It took me years to realize that Cambridge is named for the bridge over the river Cam and that Oxford is named for the ford over which the Oxen were once brought to market. The Anglo-Saxon word for mouth is 'mutha' which gives us Exmouth, Plymouth, Yarmouth, and so on, named for the places where their respective rivers give issue into the sea. The town of Shitterton is literally named for the town built on an open sewer. I will let you do your own research on the etymologies of the town of Fingringhoe in Essex and the unfortunate village of Scratch Arse Ware in Dorset, both of which always conjure up the mental image of a digit that now requires, at a minimum, a stiff wipe with a damp napkin.

Southport is another such town but not named in such a straightforward or amusing manner. The town of Southport itself was conceived when the entrepreneurial owner of the Hesketh Arms public house, a man called William Sutton, nicknamed 'The Duke' by the locals, realized the potential to cash in on the 18th-century craze of sea bathing as a curative for common ailments.

When a widow from Wigan built a cottage nearby in 1797 for seasonal lodgers, William seized on the opportunity and built a new inn on the site of the bathing house which he called the South Port Hotel. The locals thought him entirely insane and referred to the building as Duke's Folly, after all, how would potential visitors get to this sandy backwater? But William was far more astute than the yokel locals and arranged transport links from the canal located only four miles away. The Duke provided Charabanc coaches to connect his new hotel to the canal and guaranteed a steady influx of pasty-faced, sea and sun-deprived workers from the industrial mill towns of Wigan, Preston, and Manchester. Southport was born.

We met Adrian, he sat in the sunshine outside the pub on Lord Street named after the popular UK TV series, The Peaky Blinders. It was mid-afternoon on a sleepy Wednesday. The beer was cold and refreshing and we basked in the summer heat. Lord Street is adorned with broad tree-lined boulevards, glass-covered walkways, and quaint shopping arcades. It screams Victorian decadence with its water features and architectural features. It is easy to envisage ladies in petticoats and parasols strolling along to partake of the fine sea airs.

When I was a boy, the town was still gentile and pleasant. For a good while, it boasted the largest man-made lake in England, a massively popular open-air sea-bathing pool, a one-thousand-meter-long iron pier, a miniature railway, a small zoo, and a pleasure fair amongst other pleasing distractions.

The sea bathing lake has long gone, as has the zoo and the fun fair. The fountains no longer flow and graffiti mars the edifice of the marble war memorial. It quickly became apparent why the pub had chosen to name itself after the brutal Birmingham crime gangs of post-World War One Britain. We had supped only half of our pints when, with froth mustaches on our top lips, we watched as a policeman ran past. And then another. Then another, this one larger and more breathless. He came lumbering down Bold Street and entered the pub to catch his breath and ask if anybody had seen the miscreant they sought. We all shook our heads, so with a reluctant shake of his head he mopped his brow and wobbled off in pursuit of his leaner and swifter colleagues.

Ten minutes later a squad car screamed past, blues and twos blaring, heading south, followed soon after by another, similarly lit and loud, this one heading in the opposite direction. It was certainly lively for a Wednesday. I returned to our table with more drinks just in time to see two cars nearly collide, with a screech of tires, at the junction where Bold Street met Lord Street. A burly lad with heavy brows set above flinty eyes, and knuckles that reached almost to his knees got out of the car. He was clearly proud of the 0.3% of DNA that separates most of us from our Neanderthal forefathers. He approached the other driver's car to grunt angry expletives for several entertaining minutes. With his immediate rage assuaged he looked around to see, for the first time, his amused audience. Suddenly realizing we were there and enjoying his performance, he cracked his hairy knuckles loudly and menacingly took a few bow-legged steps toward us. Of course, we did what any red-blooded English folks would do. We avoided eye contact and silently studied the bubbling contents of our glasses until he got back in his car and went away.

Adrian had an appointment closer to where he lived, so he walked back towards the town center in the direction of the bus station. My phone rang and I looked up to see him come past ten minutes later waving from the top deck window. He was on his phone telling us about the street fight he had to gingerly step around in order to catch his bus.

Southport still has many good things to recommend it. Good schools and a wonderful selection of restaurants amongst them. It does its best to remain relevant by hosting wonderful events such as the annual air show and flower show, but it has become, like many Victorian seaside resorts, a pale shadow of its glorious past. Cheap air travel has robbed it of its tourists and the rich revenue it would once have brought. Many of the large department stores have gone, never to return, and every other storefront window is now either a charity shop or a coffee shop.

We only had two more nights to spend in town, and truth be told I was happy to be leaving. Given the events of the afternoon, and with a still and heavy dusk creeping across the streets, we assumed nightfall would likely bring a scene redolent of one from A Clockwork Orange. So, before Southport's equivalent of Alex DeLarge's ultra-violent switchblade-wielding '*droogs*' appeared, we proved to ourselves that Southport still had some good things to offer. We retired to a nearby restaurant to plan the next day and ate a crispy Peking duck with pancakes and Hoi-Sin sauce so good it made us tear up a little. We sat slowly chewing and shaking our heads in appreciation, seated comfortably in one of the many excellent Chinese restaurants Southport is still fortunate enough to possess.

YORKSHIRE

We left Southport on a Saturday morning, the 11th of September. The Mini was packed with our meager possessions and travel-weary puppies. We drove slowly, I was still getting used to both the Mini, and making sure I didn't inadvertently turn out of one junction and straight into oncoming traffic. My motoring brain had become a tangled cauldron of spaghetti junctions, intertwined and congealed. USA to the UK to Spain to the UK to USA to the UK, I pretended I was quite the gentlemen opening Paula's passenger door for her, when in truth I was, once more, mistakenly trying to get in the wrong side of the car. I would often find myself sitting there looking bemused as to why no steering wheel was evident and then make up some excuse for why I found myself in the passenger seat. I would mime looking for a map perhaps, checking the clove compartment for sunglasses, any reason, just in case somebody had seen me and was judging me from afar.

We also didn't have far to go, and the check-in for the Airbnb in Yorkshire was two o'clock in the afternoon. Our journey took us out of Southport on roads so painfully familiar it hurt a little. There was Oldfield's where we had bought the little red Hyundai just last year. Debenhams, closed now for good, the department store my Mum had loved to work at. We passed what used to be the British Telecom TEC depot on Crowland Street. I think TEC stood for something like Telephone Engineering Center, it's where all the big yellow lorries parked and stores could be picked up. Both me and my dad had worked there. Dad for most of his adult life, and me for four or five years early in my career. Dad would have parked his lorry around these streets, keeping out of the eyeline of the bosses and watching the clock creep towards four thirty, the time when he could safely park up for good for the weekend and hurry home for the tea that would be on the table waiting for him.

The TEC has gone now, the site has been taken over by five or six different small and shabby businesses. BT was a great place to work back in the day and everybody had fantastically creative nicknames for each other. I personally worked with 'Judge Dread', who was a part-time local magistrate. Then there was 'Burscough Bob' whose name was indeed Bob but who, puzzlingly, had, as far as anyone knew, absolutely no connection with the town of Burscough. And, of course, who could forget 'Fuck 'em all Moran', a man so embittered by life, his catchphrase had become his moniker. And lastly, Peter 'doom and gloom' McCoomb who could walk into any cheery canteen full of banter and instantly send its occupants in search of high bridges, nooses, and razor blades.

There were some BT engineer's names that had become legends across the eons of time. These are some of my favorites, gathered from across the country by friends and colleagues:

- 'Eliza' — because he Doolittle

- 'Bomb scare' — every time he walked into a telephone exchange building everybody else left.

- 'Appendix' — someone everybody could live without.

- 'Toenails' — he was so far up his manager's arse, they were the only bits of him that you could see.

- 'Badminton' — every job he did turned into a three-day event.

- 'OTIS' — he always asked for a lift on every job.

- 'Kiwi' (the flightless fitter) — he refused to climb ladders, or even use steps.

- 'Scrambler Ambler' — a poor chap whose real name was Gordon Ambler but who was inevitably immortalized when in the 1980s, he accidentally triggered a city-wide nuclear strike warning while working on a Bradford-based government telephone system.

- 'Bungalow' — he had nothing upstairs.

- 'Quarter-wit' — didn't quite make the grade of a half-wit.

- Two brothers whose real names were Simon and Brian. Unfortunately, their surname was Cortina. Forever immortalized as 'Mark One' and 'Mark Two'.

- And my personal favorite. A manager in Tyne Tees called Dave Peacock. Of course, everybody called him Chris.

My Dad's nickname was just 'mouse' he was a quiet man, not shy, just kept himself to himself, but he was liked by everybody he worked with. And before you ask, I didn't have one.

And everybody had great stories too. Working in people's homes and businesses you just get exposed to so much good material, I guess. My personal favorite that Dad told me was of a day he and his long-time work buddy, Dick Scarisbrick, were putting in new telephone cables to provide telephone service in the grounds of our local mental institution. Greaves Hall, it was called. It is now a sprawl of executive apartments or something similar. Anyway, back in the 1980's it was a large, private development with meadows and woods centered around a handsome three-story 'tudorbethan' country house with fifty-five rooms for the inmates/patients. There were some serious cases there, but most patients were allowed and encouraged to roam the grounds, and it was not unusual to meet somebody and have the strangest and most interesting of conversations with some unshaven fellow dressed only in pajamas.

The story Dad told me was that when he and Dick had finished up for the day, they loaded all of their tools and cables back on the truck, one of those with large double doors on the back, locked the truck, and set off back to the TEC depot on Crowland Street. When they got there, they had to unload the debris they had accumulated and load it up with stores for the next day. Dad parked the truck in his usual spot, walked around the back, and opened the doors. Inside were two of the inmates, silently standing, rocking backward and forwards in their striped flannels and smiling inanely at the unexpected experience of the exciting ride in the back of the big yellow lorry.

Now Dad and Dick were in the unexpected position of having inadvertently abducted two mentally ill patients. Dick made some flimsy excuse to the boss that they had forgotten something important on the site and, back in the truck, they raced back to Greaves Hall and deposited the two thoroughly baffled chaps, barefoot, in some trees just out of sight of the mansion that had become their home.

Back in the Mini, we passed through Ormskirk and then onto the M58 that used to whisk me to college in Wigan and later to work across all of Britain. We turned off the M62, the busy motorway that spans the Yorkshire Pennines and leads to all places eastern, distant, and not lightly visited. Places like Hull and Grimsby.

Our destination was a cottage in Barkisland. Paula had found it on Airbnb. Dog friendly with off-road parking and its own extensive back garden. Sat Nav took us to the place, but with it being still early, we drove past and parked for lunch at the Spring Rock Inn Pub. We had an excellent lunch and a cold pint. The menu was packed with all of the food we had missed in the USA, gammon and eggs, homemade meat pie, scampi, and chips. The staff were friendly, which is something never to be guaranteed in those parts of Yorkshire. There was plenty of covered seating and bowls of fresh water outside for the dogs. We had a lovely lunch and Paula texted the owners of the Airbnb. They were super sweet and flexible and were happy for us to arrive early.

The Airbnb was a small cottage, one of three all joined together on a long terrace and all sharing a common parking area and small yard. The cottage was upside down. A steep and startlingly squeaky staircase led to a single living room. Downstairs was one bedroom and bathroom. The bedroom had two single beds which led me to believe Paula had purposefully selected it. It was all dated with creaky and mismatched furniture. The plates and utensils looked like those my grannie's granny might have once sent to a charity jumble sale in an attempt to raise funds to buy the soldiers of the Somme a new Sopwith Camel. It also had a tiny fridge that allowed us to chill precisely one beer at a time. But it was all clean and so small, upkeep for the week and a bit we had it booked for wouldn't be a problem.

We unpacked our stuff and, needing to stretch our legs and explore the area, took the dogs out for a ramble.

Moist

I woke with a stretch in my single bed on the ground floor of the Yorkshire cottage. The sun was already streaming through the thin curtains and I could see the mini parked close by. I had slept pretty well after a fine dinner of gammon and eggs and a couple of pints of lager back at the Spring Rock Inn, but now as wakefulness replaced my dream-addled brain, I realized I was distinctly uncomfortable. I looked across at Paula who, in her single bed, was still asleep. To my dawning mind, the bed felt wet and I thought for a moment that senility and loss of my bodily functions had sneaked up on me a decade or so earlier than I had previously anticipated it would.

I pushed an arm beneath the covers and padded my hand around. It was damp everywhere, the mattress, the bedding, and to my relief my pillow. There was no way I had inadvertently released so much liquid and managed to get it so far up the head end of the bed. I got out of bed and confirmed that the cause of the moisture was merely the all-pervading dampness of the cottage itself.

The real problem was not with this particular Airbnb. It is not in fact the problem with Airbnb's in general. It is the filter that you have to apply if you are the owner of dogs. You start the search with the basics, location, and number of bedrooms. 6,000 properties of various levels of luxury at appropriately reflective prices instantly appear. Filter by off-street parking. Down to 4,000. Prefer a separate bathroom and an En-suite? Down to 2,000. Ahh but wait! You have chosen to travel with a favored canine companion or two, haven't you?

Put a cross in that box and now you have the dismal '*choice*' of two. And what a choice that has become! Where did all of the properties with hot tubs and rainfall showers go? What happened to that one with the 80" plasma tv and deep shag rug carpets close up by that cozy log burner? Of course, they are no more, because you, my friend, have chosen the companionship of a hairy, dirty, shit-making machine.

Now, please don't get me wrong. We love our dogs, both Pi and Archie, and all of the many other dogs we have had before them. Love them and adore them. They have been our choices, and the outcomes of those choices have been ours to own. But for the love of all things furry, why can't I sleep in a dry bed every now and again?

I creaked my way upstairs to the small kitchen. No matter how carefully I ascended, every step was as loud as a rifle shot. With the kettle on I yawned and opened the curtains. The view that greeted me was outstanding. The cottage was nestled between a rocky outcrop at the rear and an emerald tapestry of rolling fields crested by gleaming white wind turbines to the front.

I woke Paula with a cup of tea to ensure we were as damp on the inside as we were on the outside and then with Archie yowling his demand for his breakfast and a walk, we both got out of bed and toweled ourselves dry. We dressed, grabbed the dog's leads, and headed out for a walk to enjoy the day.

We had taken the dogs the night before but hadn't gone very far. We knew there was a moor nearby, but with the light failing we hadn't walked far enough. What we had discovered was that the back garden was steep. As in a cliff face. There was one of those little green English heritage plaques dedicated to the memory of Edmund Hillary on the wall beside the steps. The steps themselves were hand-hewn and fashioned out of discarded stone wall remnants. They led up the side of the small cliff to a small, grassy plateau covered in thick meadow. The meadow was so full of pheasants that we were constantly startled as we walked, with bird after bird breaking cover from the heavy shrubbery with a clatter of wings and its distinctive two-pitched alarm call. Archie was obsessed with them and would certainly have caught one if he was unleashed, so we had to be really careful until we were well off the property. We walked down a long dusty track, framed on either side by tumble-down ancient stone walls crowned by a thousand stinging nettles.

The three national symbols of England are the St. George's cross, the red rose, and the Three Lions crest. Incredibly noble and redolent of a country with such a rich heritage of war and brutal colonization. Did you know that on this entire planet, there exist only twenty-two countries that have not *yet* been invaded by Britain? The list isn't long so I repeat it here: Andorra, Belarus, Bolivia, Burundi, Central African Republic, Chad, Republic of Congo, Guatemala, Ivory Coast, Kyrgyzstan, Liechtenstein, Luxembourg, Mali, Marshall Islands, Monaco, Mongolia, Paraguay, Sao Tome and Principe, Sweden, Tajikistan, Uzbekistan and Vatican City.

I repeat — yet. We are coming for you Liechtenstein!

I mention it here because having relocated to England after some prolonged absence, it seems to me that the national symbols should be updated to reflect modern sensitivities and a hearty dose of reality, and stinging nettles should top the list. They are absolutely everywhere. Tough as old boots with a sting you will feel tingling for a week, they will thrive to grow five feet tall rooted on only bare concrete. You could use them to line the walls of nuclear reactors. Nettles, bluebottles and dog shit. They should be our new national symbols. Not as dramatic as lions, crosses, and roses I grant you, but plentiful and quintessentially English.

We walked across a large unmown field and then clambered over a stile set carefully into another stone wall and, magically, we were on the high moor. It was dramatic and beautiful, flowering heather mixed with gorse and yellow azalea flowers. Our footprints and paw prints were left in the sandy remains of the sandstone that was laid down in the seas of the Jurassic period and then hefted upwards across an expanse of thirty million years to form the geology we now traipsed across. Below us, we could see the dark and cramped industrial towns of Sowerby Bridge and Halifax. But around us, all around us, for as far as the eye could see, were well-trod paths through purple heather, butterflies, and the loud insectile hum of a late summer pollen harvesting, all making the most of a sun that loomed heavy in the Yorkshire sky like it never wanted to ever set again.

Trotter Towers

We tarried in Yorkshire for just over a week. It was pleasant countryside, somewhere I had previously not spent much time in. Definitely, somewhere I could return to. The challenge with Yorkshire is finding the balance between remote countryside and crowded industrial. The Dales are large and roomy, but western Yorkshire feels hemmed in and made small by the proximity of the sprawl of Halifax, Bradford, and Leeds and the never-ending encroachment of Manchester from the south.

Time had come, however for our next move. We needed to begin heading south so that we could be in closer contact with our builder and the new house that would be well under construction.

We had another AirBnB booked on a large country house estate and working farm in Oxfordshire, only a few miles from Paula's sister Kaz with whom we had sheltered the previous year while we waited for Europe to open. She had suggested we stop with her and Steve the night before so that we could get dinner and catch up, and then be within a hop, skip, and a jump of our next dog-friendly cottage. It was described as a perfect hideaway and a wonderful retreat for an aspiring writer to complete that best seller. Sorely in need of a bestseller or a seller of any kind actually, I was excited and we had booked it for three weeks. Our hopes were high.

We left Yorkshire around lunchtime on a Saturday in mid-September. The M62 was heavily congested westbound which was the way we wanted to go, around Manchester and then down the M6 to eventually join with the M40 south of Birmingham. We decided to head eastbound to join with the M1 instead. It seemed that everybody else had the same idea, as we soon joined congestion but in the opposite direction, so it was evening when we finally pulled the mini, engine tinking and popping, into the parking spot outside Kaz and Steve's house in Tetsworth.

The next morning, we headed over to check out the Airbnb. It wasn't quite what we expected. It was indeed on a country estate that was definitely still a working farm. The 'cottage' was a re-purposed farm building that remained structurally part of a large and unkempt barn. It was either an old pigsty or a cowshed. In fact, judging by the state of the carpets and soft furnishings the previous occupants had only recently vacated the premises and had wiped their trotters on the threadbare rug by the back door on their way out.

The kitchen was tiny and grubby, with mugs, knives, and forks just piled up on the disconcertingly tacky kitchen counter. You know that feeling when you walk into either a guest house or hotel or whatever? The one where you don't give a second thought to immediately start using the cups and cutlery. Well, it was the opposite of that.

The fridge was of the type found in a budget caravan and lacked even the most modest of ice compartments. Even a single cube was far beyond its capabilities.

At their very best, the British believe ice to be a rare and curiously precious commodity. I remember Paula, on a trip back to the UK to see her sisters, asking for some ice to cool the glass of warm tap water she held in her hand. As one, the three sisters turned and all said in unison.

"Ooooooohhhhh, get you? Fancy!"

Well, this fridge lacked the ability to get any perishable goods below ambient room temperature. If Jesus had been born English his best remembered parlor trick would have been turning lukewarm water into something slightly less tepid.

The electric hob had, over the span of many lifetimes achieved what IBM and Google are still trying to achieve. It had become sentient. It would boil a pan of soup furiously for twenty seconds blistering the contents firmly to the bottom of the pan, and then as soon as your back was turned, mysteriously turn itself off. Paula insisted on trying to cook a chicken for our Sunday dinner, despite my protestations that we should just go to the pub instead. She squeezed the poor bird into the narrow, and slick with the stains and juices of uncertain provenance, cavity of the oven, set the controls to Gas Mark 7, as we say here in blighty (425F to our American readers) and, pleased with the amount of heat reassuringly flooding the kitchen through the tattered and mostly missing door seal, retired to strain her eyes and give herself a migraine watching an episode of Columbo on a TV so small and lacking in color, it resembled the home screen of a Nokia 3310. An hour later she checked on the bird to find it slightly colder than when it went in.

The living room was what an estate agent might call 'bijou', but what you and I would call pokey. The room wasn't improved by having the wrought iron structure of a circular staircase dropped almost in the center. The dogs hated the staircase, it was narrow and tight and lethal if it got wet. Only the good lord knows how the pigs and cattle had got up them but from the evidence on the rugs they had somehow recently managed it.

Upstairs the decorator had decided to continue the theme of 'shabby chic' but had quickly realized that 'chic' was a far, far reach beyond both their budget and ability to execute. Spider webs hung from every surface, and water stains from recent leaks lent every wall the ambiance of an 18th-century dosshouse. The bathtub had been forced into the sharply sloping eaves, so although it technically had a shower head, the user would have to lie recumbent within the bath to make any use of it.

Everything was unfinished, dirty, antiquated, grubby, insect-ridden, filthy, and spiderwebby (spellcheck tells me that that's not a real word, but it bloody well should be). We unpacked our scant belongings and with a sigh, got to cleaning so we could at least make a cup of tea. Writer's retreat? What an original application of the phrase. I can only assume he meant as in something a writer would run, screaming, away from.

We took the dogs out for a long walk in the spectacular countryside. We had enjoyed only gorgeous unrelenting sunshine since we had arrived back, and Oxfordshire was no exception. The grounds were large with arable fields stretching far into the middle distance. Unfortunately for Pi and Archie, most of the grounds were strictly off-limits. Stark warning signs were placed at the entrance to every leafy lane and hedgerow warning of the placement of alarm mines. There were more skulls and crossbones here than on the 18th-century Spanish main. These devices use trip wires to trigger the detonation of a 12-gauge blank shotgun round. They are supposedly used as anti-poaching devices, but you couldn't shake the feeling that they were also game fully employed to keep anybody reckless enough with their hard-earned cash to stay as a guest on these grounds, strictly to the paths.

It was all very depressing and we had booked to stay at this 'perfect hideaway' for three bloody weeks.

A Train Journey

D uring the month of late September, while we languished in the luxury of Trotter Towers, somebody associated with the fuel industry leaked a government brief that warned of a shortage of heavy goods vehicle drivers. Rumors, which the popular press did absolutely nothing to dismiss, and quite openly inflamed, told of an imminent UK-wide fuel shortage. Nothing of the sort existed. Not the remotest possibility of such a thing. The UK had massive reserves of fuel and plenty of drivers to get that supply to the pumps.

Unfortunately, the rumors triggered a nationwide rush to the pumps, and every petrol tank in every town across the nation was 'topped up'. Overnight the good people of Great Britain drained every petrol station of its plentiful reserves and created the very thing that had panicked them in the first place. The shortages would last for weeks.

Luckily, we had a full tank and the Mini was nothing if not frugal. On the downside, we had agreed to drive to Somerton, mid-week, to meet with Jim the developer, and Pete the builder, to see how our new house was looking. A return drive to Somerton would pretty much empty our tank.

I did some research and found that Reading had a direct mainline train service to Castle Cary, only a short taxi drive away from where we needed to be. We booked a room and dinner combo at the White Hart Inn, the poshest place to stay in Somerton, and one surprisingly cold morning we dropped the dogs off at Kaz's house and drove to Reading train station.

It's really strange growing up in a country and spending a good deal of your adult life there and then moving to another country for fifteen years. All of a sudden, we had no idea how things like train stations worked. I had tickets safely downloaded on my phone but the security gates at the bottom of the long escalator which led up to the platforms seemed to be automated. I waved the phone and its QR codes vaguely across what seemed to be a scanner but nothing happened. Finally, some bored-looking British Rail operative took pity on us, manually opened the barrier, and waved us through.

We purchased what might have been the most dispiritingly arid bacon roll in the UK, from the only outlet open in the vast airy station concourse. So bereft of flavor and substance was it that we both ended up choking on ingested crumbs, it was like eating Jacob's cream crackers straight out of the crinkly orange packet.

We looked for a waste bin to deposit the remnants in, but there wasn't one to be seen anywhere. The genius-level logic here is that by removing all of the bins, would-be terrorists would be deprived of a handy hiding place in which to hide their explosive devices. Of course, what it really achieves is to deprive people trying to innocently dispose of their inedible sandwiches, of a suitably clean and sanitary receptacle in which to do so.

The train arrived and we took our pre-booked seats. I always enjoyed train travel when I worked in the UK. Every year I drove in excess of one hundred thousand miles, up and down the congested motorways of Britain. The train to London, or occasionally Glasgow, was a rare treat. My reward for such indulgence was a full English breakfast (I was on expenses back then), a comfy seat, and an ever-changing view of the English countryside.

The best bit was on the slow approach to a station, where you always get a secretive peek through the kitchen windows of some of the terrace houses that butt up against the railway lines. A tiny fleeting glimpse of lovely normal working-class people padding around in bare feet, rubbing sleep from their eyes, busy making cups of tea in dressing gowns while they lived out their lives in houses where alarm clocks were made entirely obsolete due to windowpanes that would rattle madly when the express blatted through at seven-thirty every morning. It was the only way to travel.

Our train was an express direct from London, it only stopped at Reading, where we caught it, Newbury racecourse, Pewsey, Westbury, and our destination of Castle Cary. The train streaked through the rolling countryside. A lovely man with a trolley full of choccies and fizzy drinks ambled through the carriages and we arrived completely relaxed only fifty-one minutes later.

It's still shocking to me to hear people moan and whine about the cost and tardiness of Britain's railway system. To be fair we only use it now and again so are far from experts, but you can literally get to most large towns at very reasonable prices and generally on time and in great comfort. They even give you money back these days for every minute the train is late, which essentially means that they are free.

In the 1950's you could get directly to a great many more places. Indeed, prior to 1964, we could have got the train directly to Somerton. Unfortunately, somebody in the government put a zealot called Doctor Richard Beeching in charge of investigating why the railways were losing a little money. His answer, based on extremely dubious and biased data (he took many measures of passenger usage at night and across weekends), was to close 7,000 miles of track, terminate 2,128 stations and make 67,000 railway worker jobs redundant.

Surely, not everything in life needs to be hugely profitable. Some things are for the good of the people the government pretends to serve. Some reports suggest that all of Beeching's cuts saved only a paltry £30 million.

The cuts were also astoundingly short-sighted. In the 1950's, UK car journeys consumed only 100 billion passenger kilometers per year. That figure is now over 700 billion and the roads and towns they pass through are dirty and congested as a result. Like many other rural towns, Somerton is now in discussions with the government to have its station re-instated, but even if it is approved, it certainly won't happen in my lifetime and the cost to do so will be on the scale where gasts quickly become flabbered.

We met the taxi we had reserved in the Castle Cary car park and with the odd mixture of casual xenophobia and off-color politics that the typical British cabbie seems compelled to share, we made the fifteen-minute journey to Somerton. Incidentally, the eleven-mile taxi ride cost us more than the ninety-mile train journey, by a substantial margin (and there was no trolley service).

We checked into the White Hart and with our bags stowed we were eager to see how close to habitable the new house was. We had a meeting with Jim and Pete in under an hour and we were keen to take a look. We bought a 'Glastonbury' pastie from the charmingly named Burns the Bread, the local baker's shop, and with crumbs on our chins, we walked through the village in the direction of Rose Cottage, which was the cottage we had rented the previous year.

As we approached the building site, I remember craning my neck and squinting into the distance to see if I could spot the signs of the red roof tiles I fervently hoped would be in place. Unfortunately, if there was a roof, it had yet to be hoisted onto the unfinished pile of stone that would be our house. No doors, no windows, no roof, and as far as we could see no builders.

We walked around the back of the property and failed to see anybody, working or otherwise, so we waded through the mud of what would end up as the shared courtyard. We stepped around piles of rubble and around a bright yellow earth mover. The back of the house was entirely open to the elements. The floors hadn't been poured and the cement that glued the damp breeze blocks together was still drying. It was clear that this house had a very long way to go to be habitable. As we stood, eyes wide in despair an Irish voice called out to us.

"Hey you! What are you doing here?"

We turned to find an angry Irishman, dressed in a donkey jacket and Hi-Viz jerkin and muddy wellies walking sharply towards us.

"We are the Wareing's. We have a meeting with Jim here in an hour or so."

"Oh, sorry," he said, "we've had a lot of nosey bastards poking around the site recently. Excuse my language," he added realizing we were the paying customers who had come to meet his boss.

"It's OK. Is Jim here?"

"I'll get him for you," he paused, for the first time noticing our pale faces and stricken eyes as we looked on in despair at the muddy grey building site that should have been our home in only a few weeks.

"It's not as bad as it looks," he added.

PACHYDERMS

B ack at the White Hart, we had dinner and mused over our
meeting with Jim. It hadn't gone great. Jim was apologetic,
his suppliers and contractors had let him down, timber was in short
supply, and one small slip on the timeframe had led to another one,
COVID had caused delays due to sickness, yadda, yadda, yadda.

It wasn't that the reasons for the delays were untrue. It was all
just very frustrating, and now we would soon be homeless again.
Before we left the site, we asked Jim to be open and honest about the
timescale to get the house finished and us moved in—the very worst
of all worst-case scenarios if you will. We all agreed that at the end of
November, by the very latest the first week of December, we would be
in.

The next morning, we took the train back to Reading and, with
a light foot on the gas pedal of the Mini, we drove back, past empty
gas station after empty gas station. Each pump on the forecourt wore
a fluttering plastic supermarket shopping bag on its head with black
and yellow hazard tape strung between. An hour later we arrived in

Tetsworth to pick up the dogs from Kaz's house. We lingered for way too long, reluctant to go back to our idyll in the country, the one we shared with the livestock. Kaz told us that she and Steve had rented a cottage for a week or so and would be happy for us to have their house while they were away. We jumped at the chance. Their return would also signal the end of our time in Oxfordshire.

Paula found a new pet-friendly Airbnb in Somerton, timed for a mid-October arrival, just a few weeks away. We thought it would be perfect timing to be local, just in time to supervise the final build of the house and finally get back in the right area, so that we could order beds and all the other household items we would need for our move-in.

We had heard that the delivery times for sofas were in the order of months, so with our move-in looming, we decided to go shopping and get one ordered. We went back to Reading and found an L-section sofa we liked. It was in a department store on one of those shopping lots where the space is 80% car park and where the city planners deem it compulsory to also have a KFC outlet in situ. With the sofa chosen, we just needed a thirty-minute mental timeout before our signatures made the final financial commitment and, with it being the only place with a public toilet, we ended up walking across to it now.

I am not sure that 'good' is the correct adjective here, but it was certainly finger-licking. Twenty-two napkins later and with the grease smeared across knuckles and noses, we walked back, stomachs grumbling, and bought the sofa. Their earliest delivery was in February.

Finally, the day rolled around and we were forced to leave our lovely writer's retreat. Without a single backward glance, we slammed the door and I spun the wheels of the Mini on the gravel, thrilled to finally be out of the place. We felt cleaner and more contented immediately. We drove to Kaz's house and deposited some of our surplus things in

Steve's garage (again) and once more, dogs piled and panting on the backseats, we hit the road.

It was quite thrilling. Our last Airbnb, and this last one back in Somerton, which was the town we actually wanted to be in. Paula had found a little three-story cottage right behind the church and located just off Cow Square, so named because it is where the cows were paraded when being auctioned in centuries past. It would be quite a guilty pleasure to have the livestock outside the house for a change.

The drive was fast and easy. We passed the Mini factory located on the ring road Southeast of perennially crowded and congested Oxford. Smart and expansive Victorian detached houses were pressed up against the dual carriageway. At one time, perhaps prior to Doctor Beeching getting involved in the railways, these would have been immensely desirable homes. Large gardens and private drives that once led onto a leafy tree-lined street. Now their handsome wrought iron garden gates are inches from the endless traffic that has overwhelmed Oxford. The city has sprawled under its own success and the imposing gravitas of its esteemed university, the oldest in the English-speaking world.

Science parks and educational institutes have proliferated, but it has become a far cry from the serenity portrayed by the British TV series 'Morse', or the city of dreaming spires described in Matthew Arnold's Victorian poem 'Thyrsis'. Indeed, a more accurate representation of today's Oxford would have Inspector Morse broken down by the roadside with the bonnet of his 1960s burgundy Jaguar Mark II propped open, smoke billowing from the overheating engine as articulated lorries bellowed past, inches from the leather elbow patches of his corduroy jacket.

On to the A34. For as long as I can remember this long stretch of dual carriageway has been jammed with trucks. It's a shortcut between the M40 and the M4, and heavy goods vehicles are often sprawled across both lanes, playing convoy and ponderously pretending that they can overtake each other. So it was with some relief that we finally joined the A303 and turned west towards leafy Wiltshire and then onward to even sleepier Somerset. We passed Stonehenge and Paula took the compulsory picture on her iPhone as the traffic slowed, partly due to the road here going down to a single lane and because people, no matter how many times you have seen the monoliths suddenly loom over the sloping meadow, just love to marvel at the mystery and extreme age of the stones...and take a picture.

We arrived at the cottage mid-afternoon and with the car parked two wheels on the pavement outside, we bundled the dogs and our belongings hurriedly inside. The cottage was everything that Trotter Towers was not. Clean modern kitchen with sparkling appliances, spacious bedrooms with two gleaming white bathrooms. Every surface had been disinfected; every carpet was freshly vacuumed.

The only elephant in the room was the couch. From every angle, it resembled a vast, olive green, wrinkle-skinned pachyderm that had been shot with a large caliber directly between the eyes and fallen, legs akimbo to fill the small space of the living room. It was vastly uncomfortable in the way that only the British can brush off with pleasantries such as "it is what it is," and "mustn't grumble."

Not a single part of the couch would be molded into a shape that could, for more than a minute, support the frame of a human or canine occupant. The cushions had been stuffed with goose feathers, but the feathers had long since escaped leaving only the pointy quills behind. Once sat upon, the cushions all slowly moved, like lumpy glaciers across a frozen tundra of itchy burlap, to gradually reposition us awkwardly into back achingly recumbent contortions. If the designers had wanted their customers to be hugely uncomfortable, just not immediately, it was a glorious testament to their mastery of engineering.

Vying for its lack of comfort was the square footage it consumed. It filled every spare inch of the living room. The front door cleared the back of the couch by a bare half an inch. To get a cup of tea from the kitchen to the couch required horizontal gymnastics and hips far more subtle than the old creaky ones we possessed.

We also soon became obsessed with parking. There was no private space in which to secure the Mini. All of the residents of Broad Street competed nightly for the closest spots to their respective houses. During the day, businesses added their vehicles to further fuel the fission of excitement of returning from the shops with a car filled with frozen chickens and tins of soup. The parking spot outside the opticians, right next to Cow Square became known as, and still is in my mind, pole position, it being the closest possible to our little cottage.

With all of our few things safely stored, we began to think about what we would need for the new house when it became habitable in just a few weeks. We found ourselves once more in the odd predicament of being folks in our mid-50s, who had worked their entire lives, and yet owned no furniture, no beds, mattresses or bedding, no cutlery or dishware, no cooking utensils or patio furniture. It all needed to be purchased, and either shipped to the new house when the garage was made weatherproof or stored somewhere else.

It was late October now and the weather was beginning to shift from warm and showery to mild and showery. Before we knew it, it would soon be cold and showery. The British are never short of a conversation to be had about the fucking weather, but the central themes are nothing if not tediously consistent.

The cottage was already packed with even our meager belongings, so I began the search for a lockup or storage unit. I emailed a few places, some were full, and others just didn't respond. I did get an instant response from a lady called Jane in the nearby town of Curry Rivel so we made an appointment to go see her the next day.

When we got there, we chatted for a while about how warm/mild/cold it had been and was going to be, and established precisely how showery the weather had been recently, before we were shown the storage lockers. Jane was old-school Glastonbury, which means hippy to you and me. It's as much an attitude as an appearance, and it's a popular vibe in this here Somerset part of the world. Glastonbury is home to the mystical Tor, and as much as the blood of a scientific atheist runs in my veins, there is something undeniably Arthurian about the Tor itself and the landscape it dominates. It has been a draw to the disenfranchised, the esoteric, and the good old-fashioned mentally ill for a thousand years, and the huge annual music festival has done nothing but multiply their numbers.

The Glastonbury festival or 'Glasto' as it is known in Somerset, began as a loose grouping of 1500 people in a field on Worthy Farm just outside the town of Glastonbury. It was the brainchild of Michael Eavis in 1970. The first headliners were The Kinks, Wayne Fontana, and T-Rex when they were still called Tyrannosaurus Rex. It now attracts up to 300,000 people across five days, entertaining the festival goers from nearly one hundred stages, powering speakers through the consumption of 650,000 Watts, and collecting the contents of bowels in 2,000 toilets, which is precisely 2,000 toilets too few.

The first time we visited Glastonbury, we parked the car in Silver Street, and while Paula popped a pound coin and a fifty pence piece into the Pay as you Go parking meter a wizard walked by. Now, this wasn't some guy with a false beard and a robe heading to a festival or fancy-dress party. This was a chap who donned his purple robes embroidered in bright glittering stars, put on his pointy hat, and grabbed his gnarled hazel walking stick every morning, in precisely the same way that most of us put on our shoes, tie a tie, and grab our laptop bag before leaving the house. It's just not unusual here. Witches and Wiccans mix with the general population, bank tellers, and shop assistants, with cordiality and ease.

On the same trip, we stopped by the mobile fishmonger and bought some fresh salmon. Next to us was a pretty young woman with a bicycle that had a baby carriage secured behind it. We both looked to see and admire her baby and perhaps make a cooing noise, so we were a little surprised to see not a baby but a rabbit. It's what goes for normal down here.

Jane showed us the locker, a huge green corrugated steel ship container type of unit, the sort we see on storage wars. The door and the lock mechanism were complicated and reassuringly heavy and the inside of the unit was bone dry and several degrees warmer than the showery outside. We had brought a rug and box of random bits and bobs that were cluttering up the cottage. We signed the month-by-month contract telling Jane we would only need it for a month, two at the most, paid our deposit, and leaving our paltry items, lonely in the far corner of the unit, we swung the heavy doors closed. I had never had a storage unit before and drove away with a stupidly childish grin on my face. With room to store our crap, we could let the buying commence.

Oxfordshire

The cottage didn't have a garden, so every morning Paula would slip Wellington boots on her bare feet and pull her heavy winter coat over her pajamas and take the dogs out into the churchyard so they could pee and poop. At night, before we went to bed it would be my turn to walk in the moonlight among the tumbled gravestones. You could find me every night, bare legs beneath the hem of my wax Barbour jacket, breath steaming in the chill of the night, muttering like a crazy person, "wee wees, wee wees, oh come on for Christ's sake, wee wees already!"

The 13th-century church has a bell tower that, when it's not game-fully employed calling the faithful to their knees on a Sunday morning, peals the hour and every quarter-hour, and its sudden reverberations made me jump on more than one occasion as I crushed frost grimed grass underfoot, and sought to avoid stepping on the remains of some ancient last testament to a former resident of the former capital city of Wessex.

During the day we walked the dogs through the village and past the construction site. There remained very little progress. Pete was always around and would give us a cheery daily update as to the things he wanted to complete this week but which almost unfailingly did not in fact get done.

"The roof trusses are coming tomorrow, that'll only take a day."

"Ok."

"The chippies are on site tomorrow to frame the interior walls, that'll only take another day."

"Great."

"The roofers are booked for the end of the week."

"Let me guess?"

"Yes, another day," a pause to consider the time and complexity of such a task, "maybe two."

Every conversation ended with a reassuring wink and what was quickly becoming his catchphrase delivered in his lilting Irish brogue, "Honest to God, it's not as bad as it looks."

We would walk past again at the end of the week to see Pete standing forlornly alone on the muddy site with the house sans roof and interior walls. It was actually harder being so physically close to the build. Even when we didn't walk up the drive of the development, we couldn't help craning our necks to see if somebody, anybody was on the scaffolding, doing something...anything. All we could hear was the silence of hammers not striking nails.

In the meantime, we began to order everything we would need should the house ever get completed. Some from Amazon, some from the local shops, almost every day we received something, a mattress, a bedframe, some storage units, a set of plates. We tested the carrying capabilities of the little Mini, piling stuff into it, and seats down, Paula scrunched awkwardly in the back seat as we made trip after trip to our storage unit in Curry Rivel. Slowly, piece by piece the unit began to fill up.

October slipped slowly into November, and soon enough we were walking to the playing fields to watch our first bonfire night celebration in many years. There was almost no progress on the house and finally, we got a call from Jim that we already knew must be coming. There was no chance of hitting the end of November deadline, but...we absolutely, definitely, had no chance of not being, would be in the house in time to comfortably celebrate our first Christmas.

With the couch still not coming until February, if we did move into the new house, we faced a Christmas sitting on the floor, so we cleverly ordered some patio furniture that would serve as an emergency dining table and chairs. The real, and imminent problem facing us was that our booking of the AirBnB was due to end on the last day of November. Somebody else had booked it for three weeks so it wasn't available again until December 21st. We would soon be homeless again.

Kaz as always stepped up and offered that we could journey back to Oxfordshire and stay a few weeks with her. The Airbnb in Somerton was available to rent again from December 21st so we booked it again, this time for a month. If the house did indeed get finished for Christmas, fantastic, we might lose some of our deposit money on the Airbnb, but we felt, deep down, that Jim's idea of progress, and the one we witnessed every day on our dog walks, were as far apart as Democrats and Republicans, or perhaps as far apart as the cupboard that stores the spare toilet rolls from where you are sat. Best to give him a generous additional three weeks, plenty of time to get the house finished. We didn't tell Jim or Pete of course, best to keep the pressure turned up as high as we could.

So, one frosty morning, on the last day of November we had the Mini boot up and all the seats down as we once again piled our worldly possessions and beloved, but quickly greying pups into the back of the car. The day before we had gone back to the storage container and emptied the cottage of anything superfluous to our needs for the next three weeks. Still, the Mini did soon floweth over so to speak, and we had to shoehorn the remainder of our belongings and some gifts for a planned early Christmas, around the already uncomfortable dogs.

As we finished packing, the owners of the Airbnb showed up to clean. We were definitely running late, but they were kind and chatted to us as we finished packing. We may have mentioned the unsatisfactory state of the green couch to them and they immediately went on the defensive.

"Well, it was *very* expensive when we bought it."

"Many guests *remark* on it."

"*Most* people say they enjoy it."

This is the problem with short-term lets as opposed to long-term rentals. People can put up with almost anything for a long weekend, especially when you are intent on enjoying precious vacation time with your family. Even truly vulgar and expensive items age to the point where they need to be retired, just look at Donald Trump and Joe Biden. Something genuinely awful can quickly and easily become a thing that can be 'remarked' upon. Watching your eighty-five-year-old granny struggling in vain to escape from the clutch of the ever-shifting cushions can be something the rest of the family can enjoy, as they wipe tears of hilarity from their eyes, as long as the poor old dear only has to suffer it a few times across a space of days.

When you rent for several weeks, you get a very different perspective. We left, even as they thanked us, through gritted teeth, for our overly honest feedback, Paula helpfully shouting, "no, honestly, *burn* it!" out of the window as we sped away.

Another Somerton Xmas

B ack in Tetsworth, we settled in for our few weeks' respite from having to witness the daily lack of progress on the house. Christmas was coming swiftly, and while Steve was working away most of the time in Edinburgh, we went shopping in Wycombe and Thame for a planned early Christmas dinner we planned to hold at Kaz's house prior to our return to Somerton.

Our COVID vaccination status had once more risen its head. We had both received one shot in the UK and we had received two shots in the USA. Because of the move between countries, our NHS records showed that, even though we had received a total of three bruised arms, our status was that we were incomplete and needed another. We called into our doctor's office and flapped our Walgreen vaccination records under their noses, but much like the USA they were unable to recognize them as something that could be transferred onto the NHS system of record. We needed another one.

We booked into a center in Slough and drove there early one morning. Slough is a soulless place. It's an industrial town, the one chosen by Ricky Gervais for the location of his history-making mockumentary 'The Office,' presumably because it mirrors the show's themes of social clumsiness and despair. We found the vaccination center in the grounds of a sports hall and, with barely any queues we were in and out with another sore arm and back in the Mini in thirty minutes. We stopped for an instantly forgettable lunch in some pub on the way home and coming too fast off the M40, I turned onto the B4009 and went straight through a mobile speed camera traveling at seven miles an hour faster than I should have been, earning me three points and a £100 fine. Great day out for all.

On our previous trip to the UK, when we rented in Somerton for eight months, we purchased a rather swanky treadmill. It was one of the items Steve had picked up in the rented van. Kaz was kindly intent on returning it to us. So, now we faced the dilemma of how to get it back to Somerton in a Mini. With Paula and Kaz out shopping, I borrowed some of Steve's tools and set to work. It didn't come apart easily but I managed, with skinned knuckles, to get it into four or five large pieces. The actual running deck and motor were by far the largest. I carefully measured each component and then, back outside with all of the Mini doors open, I calculated that it would just fit. Nobody in the Mini with the treadmill would be remotely comfortable, but if we rubbed butter on all of the internal surfaces and all sat squashed, noses against the windscreen, we could get it in and back to our storage container.

The next morning, with the taste of bacon on our lips and brown sauce in my gray beard, we managed to force the component parts of the treadmill into the surprisingly Tardis-like space of the Mini. Pressed up against its hard edges we contorted ourselves around whatever limited space remained and set off. The plan was to drive straight to Curry Rivel, drop off the treadmill, meet with Pete to see how the house was progressing, get lunch at the Globe, and drive straight back to Tetsworth. It's a two-hundred-and-fifty-mile round trip and with all the stops we needed to make, would take us most of the day.

We arrived at the storage container around eleven in the morning and with the engine popping we slowly uncoiled ourselves, extricated cramped limbs from beneath the angular steel edges of the treadmill, and stood in the frigid air, stamping life into numbed hands and feet. Paula fiddled with the locks and opened the doors. The space in the once-empty cavernous unit was really filling up. We now owned two mattresses, two bedframes, although one was hopefully in our garage on the new build, sets of plates, patio furniture, cups, cutlery, and all sorts of mystery-boxed items, the contents of which had temporarily slipped from memory. We made some space and piece by piece laid the components of the treadmill on the floor.

We reconfigured the Mini to make it more habitable for human life, drove back to Somerton and parked the Mini on West Street. The house we had bought was the mid-terrace of a row of three. Normally when we walked the dogs, we always approached the house from the rear where, when it is finished, there will be a courtyard with private parking spaces. Today, we walked with our hearts in our mouths back down the street to approach from the front of the house.

A flutter of surprise and elation greeted us. A Christmas miracle! A roof! Fully tiled, glowing red in the low winter sunshine. There were windows, with glass in, and there was the bright blue front door we had ordered months ago, actually in a door frame and closed against the elements. Our spirits were lifted and we stepped lightly around the corner, smiles creasing the corner of our mouths to meet with Pete. Our elation was sadly short-lived. The rear of the property told a very

different story. The roof at the back of the property had a scattering of tiles but most of it was the familiar waterproof green plastic
membrane, fluttering and snapping in the wind. The scaffolding was
deserted and the back of the house was still open to the elements.

Pete walked up as we stood staring, to utter his now famous catchphrase which was beginning to haunt us. It was December 14th. Fac-
toring in the break for Christmas, with no builders on site the week
before and most of the week after, even our pessimistic plan of having
the Airbnb until January 21st was looking wildly optimistic. Add to
that, the fact that Pete was entirely on his own on the site. There
was nobody else working on anything, no electricians, no roofers, no
chippies, no nobody. With a sigh of resignation, we told Pete we would
call Jim for the official update and went for lunch.

Back in Testsworth, we held our early Christmas dinner on the
night of the 20th December. We had a lamb roast dinner cooked by
Paula and Kaz and exchanged a few presents. The next morning, we
drove, once more back to Somerton. Pole position was empty when
we arrived so we quickly emptied the car. With hope in our hearts that
the owners had taken our feedback to heart and burnt the monstrous
green sofa, we opened the front door. But there was Nelly in all of her
emerald elephantine wrinkled glory.

Christmas was a very quiet affair. We had another lamb dinner
listening to the bells of St Michael & All Angels' Church ringing
madly in our ears. We spoke to Adam on WhatsApp, pulled a cracker
or two, and had an early night.

The call with Jim failed to offer much positive news. He seemed to
finally admit defeat. There was no chance of the house being finished
before our time in the Airbnb expired. We met with Jim and Pete
onsite again on the 11th of January and while there had been some
progress, the roof was finally tiled and the chippies had begun to frame

up the rooms, and the first fix had been mostly done for plumbing, and electrics, work of truly Himalayan proportions remained to be completed.

Jim very kindly offered us the use of an Airbnb that he owned in Kingsand, Cornwall. We would probably only need it for a week or so in any event, so he had blocked it out for a month to make absolutely sure. We paid him one pound to make the contract tight and signed the paperwork.

KINGSAND

During the week leading up to our departure from Somerton, we did several cold and rainy runs between the cottage and the storage unit. We, once more, stripped our belongings down to what we could safely transport in the Mini, alongside the dogs, and deposited what remained alongside the treadmill and mattresses, bed frames, and patio furniture, in the increasingly crowded unit.

The morning of the 21st January we walked the dogs down to the building site. Pete was there and at last, there were some signs of activity on the house. We took a last look around the site. It was a shame we would miss the last, and most interesting, part of the build. We had been in, or close to, Somerton since mid-October. It had been an expensive place to rent a cottage, but we had wanted to be close to the build so that we could check on progress (snort), and make sure the house got finished precisely how we wanted it. Now when that looked to be close to actually happening, we would be miles away in Cornwall. Pete reassured us once more that nothing was as bad as anything looked, we played the role we had adopted in pretending to believe him, said our farewells, and told him we would see him in a few weeks.

With the dogs walked and the car filled to the gunwales, every inch crammed with boots and coats, dog leads and bowls, we squeezed ourselves into what little space remained and once more hit the road.

The trip was fast for the most part and the weather was fair, chilly but not so showery as it might have been. We drove over the Tamar River on the new Tamar Bridge. The modern bridge runs adjacent to the Royal Albert Bridge which was built by Isambard Kingdom Brunel himself. The original bridge was completed in 1859, the same year that its esteemed designer died and his name was placed on two plates on either end of the bridge to commemorate his life. The old bridge is one of those bridges you see in movies, scenic calendars, and on postage stamps and never actually know where it is. Well, now you do.

We turned onto the Rame Peninsula that faces Portsmouth and points like an accusatory crooked finger across the English Channel towards Northern France. As we did so the roads immediately narrowed. Flashes of the sea, blue and foam-flecked could be glimpsed between the tall hedgerows, and we were forced to pull hard to the side as the occasional delivery truck barreled past us.

We finally arrived at the turn-off for Kingsand. The approach road to the village is a long, narrow single-lane stretch of road that runs from the top of the hill all the way down to the beach and car park at the bottom. The houses crowd the road on either side, with pavements for pedestrians mostly absent. Front doors open almost directly onto the streets. The same road is used for getting into the village and also getting out. We were there out of season; it must have been hell to navigate in the summer months.

Of course, the day we arrived the road was blocked by roadworks. There was no other way down to Jim's house which lay almost at the bottom of the hill, so we drove around the barriers and made our way carefully down the steep hill. We counted house numbers as we went. Perhaps Cornwall has a different interpretation of ordinal numbers and the sequence in which they typically appear, but first, they counted down, as was expected, but then halfway down, for a reason that eludes us still, they began to count back up again. It mattered not, as only a few doors from Jim's cottage a contractor's truck drove out of the car park at the bottom and headed at speed towards us, forcing me to scramble for the gears and reverse all the way back up the bloody hill.

With him gone, we tried once more. We had to block the street to unload the car and then with the same contractor's truck now impatiently behind me, trying to return to the hole in the street they had dug up, I moved the car to the car park and walked back up the hill to the house.

The house was as lovely as we knew it would be. A large lounge with wood burning fire, spacious well-equipped kitchen, and lots of bedrooms upstairs. We picked the best one and settled in and walked to the little shop at the bottom of the hill to get some lunch. Having lived in the UK for a good part of my formative years I had continually been told of the glory of a real Cornish pastie. For the American's out there, the pastie is a circular shaped pastry filled with meat and potatoes, and then folded and sealed with a thick crimped edge to form a semi-circle of goodness. The legend is that 18th-century Cornish Tin and Copper miners would hold the crimped crust in their dirty, soiled hands and feast on the clean contents within.

Everything in Cornwall is special and this is made evident by placing the word Cornish in front of all consumables. Cornish cheese is the creamiest, Cornish milk is the freshest, Cornish honey the sweetest and the Cornish Hen is an American variety of a broiler chicken, so very little to do with Cornwall at all. I really don't know why I mentioned it.

We ordered a couple of Cornish pasties for lunch and I have to confess it was, by a significant order of magnitude the best thing I have eaten for a very long time. It had the advantage that it repeated on me throughout the remainder of the day so I got to enjoy it over and over and over again, as did every person within three feet of me.

Kingsand is actually a twin town with neighboring Cawsand. To you and me they appear to be a single village, but before the boundary changes of 1844, Kingsand was recognized as being in Devon, and Cawsand being located in Cornwall. The residents of the two villages were proud of their respective counties and competition was rife between the two. The Halfway House Inn is situated on the old boundary but both parts of the village are now considered to be in Cornwall, regardless of what the locals might tell you.

If you are on holiday there, the place is spectacular. A tiny fishing village, with a rich history of smuggling, with houses nestled in the crags and rocks that tumble down to the beaches. But we were out of season and much of the village had been bought by folks who lived elsewhere and only used the properties for vacations in the summer months. Most were empty and the businesses closed, waiting for the tourists to return.

Of the four pubs, only the Halfway House was fully open. The Devonport was totally closed, the Rising Sun was open on limited days only and the Cross Keys had a large and unfriendly sign outside that made it clear you were not welcome if you ended up in the unfortunate position, that we all occasionally end up in, of needing to empty a bulging bladder. I can't imagine this was a major inconvenience to the landlord, as public toilets, always open and well maintained, were available only twenty feet away across the square. As if to clarify to all and sundry what a miserable bastard he was, the Landlord had also posted that dinner was served until seven in the evening after which time you could just fuck off home.

We ordered groceries to be delivered, as the supermarkets were distant and difficult to get to. We even had to specify a small delivery vehicle as the roads were so narrow. The house had a courtyard garden and neither Pi nor Archie relished using it as a toilet, so we ended up having to either take them down to the beach or up the steep hill to the promontory that overlooked the bay. Both options meant the pajamas and wellies again, although I have to admit that the scenery was as spectacular as any place in the world to view the sun breaking cover of the land to throw its first dazzling reflection on the breaking waves while watching a dog crouch on shaking legs to curl one out.

The village sits right on top of the Southwest coastal path. The path stretches for 630 miles (1,014 km), running from Minehead in the north of Somerset, all along and around the coasts of Devon and Cornwall, to finally reach its end in Poole Harbor in Dorset. We did several day hikes, and the elevation changes made it a fun challenge. It has been calculated that the totality of the path has an elevation change of 114,931 ft (35,031 m), which is almost four times the height of Mount Everest, although we only did a small hillock worth in comparison. It was also wonderful to unexpectedly come across a few of the wild ponies, close at hand, that are encouraged to munch on the bracken which then allows the wildflowers to grow.

As beautiful as it was, and how lovely it was to be a literal skimming stone's throw from the beach and the ever-changing sea, we soon became bored. The village of Kingsand is lovely for a long weekend. Three or four days, even a week perhaps, but the days were slipping by us again, January transitioning into February, while we impatiently waited for news of the house. We felt trapped in an incredibly picturesque prison, stir-crazy, we walked the dogs and then with nothing else to do we went out again to walk ourselves to fatigue. In the afternoons we drank tea while watching Tipping Point and the Chase on TV until it was time to cook dinner and then go to bed, again and again, day after day.

A welcome break for us was a visit by a couple of friends, Bret and Julie from Somerton. They came for four or five days and we made a trip to the pub (not the Cross Keys) and even made it out to the Eden Project for the day, which was great fun, except Paula made me ice skate. When I say ice skate, I wobbled around the rink in a painfully slow and ever-decreasing circle while I made useful windmills out of my arms. Still, I didn't fall and fracture a hip which, as I first stumblingly took to the ice, seemed to be the most likely outcome. And I was at least faster than two or three of the toddlers there who held onto giant plastic skating penguins.

The Eden Project itself is comprised of two huge enclosures consisting of adjoining domes that house thousands of plant species. From afar they look like gargantuan golf balls upended into the ground, dominating the landscape for miles. Each dome emulates a natural biome, a rainforest biome, and a Mediterranean biome. The site is an old clay pit that, before construction began, was used by the BBC as the planet surface of 'Magrathea' in the 1981 TV series adaptation of The Hitchhiker's Guide to the Galaxy. It is really impressive, and if you are in the area you should go. It really helps if you like plants a LOT though.

While Bret and Julie stayed, storm Eunice also visited. Bringing sustained winds of over 81mph and one record-breaking gust of 122mph, it made one of the evenings memorable for everybody. The day started with our usual walk along the beach and already we could all feel the winds picking up, we all squinted and protected our eyes as sand was whipped up by the gales and stingingly blasted into our faces. The bay was normally littered with boats, small fishing smacks, and even the occasional warship from the naval base in Plymouth, but one by one they were all moved to behind the artificial concrete bar that guards the entrance to the Tamar. By evening we sheltered in the house with a wood fire blazing in the hearth playing board games, and through the night we could hear the frenzied winds howling around the brick edges of the building and plucking at the roof tiles.

Finally, we got a call from Pete. He had lost our choice of bathroom tiles; the ones we had picked out way back in September I think, and we needed to pick out new ones.

"When do you need them by?" It was Wednesday morning.

"I need to order them tomorrow to pick them up on Friday."

For fuck's sake, I thought. *We have been sitting here doing nothing for weeks and now we need to find a tile store in the middle of nowhere and pick out something nice on twenty-four hours' notice.*

Of course, I didn't say that, and at least it sounded like good news. There was finally a surface in the house that could be tiled!

"OK, Pete. We'll let you know what we like tomorrow."

The next day we found a store on the outskirts of Exeter, almost two hours away (everything is two hours from Kingsand), and drove back across the Torpoint bridge in the direction of home, spending two pounds on the toll. It felt great to be back across the bridge, a real day out. It gave the impression of going home, a dress rehearsal for a time that over the last few weeks began to feel like it would never happen. We had both lost sight of why we were even in the UK by that point. The new house seemed impossibly far away.

We picked out a white tile design that had a shimmery opalescent effect. It was understated but classy and, back in the car park we texted Pete our choice and then drove the two hours back to the house.

Pete called us up again a few days later. The house would be ready for us on the 11th of March. The painters would still be on site, and we had no garden, but it would be just about habitable. We were beyond ecstatic, and elated, we began to drive our stock of tins and frozen goods down, to empty the larder and the freezer. We planned the drive home and did a practice pack of the Mini. I carried two-pound coins for the toll bridge with me everywhere I went, desperately ready to leave.

One thing our stay in that beautiful place had convinced us of. Neither one of us wanted to live in what sometimes appears to be a dream location. These sleepy Cornish and Devon villages with the steep roads that tumble to the ocean sell a vision of tranquility and charm, and perhaps that is the case for some people. People who don't like people perhaps, but it wasn't for us and we craved the comparable metropolis that is actually the sleepy hamlet of Somerton.

We were all set to leave Jim's house that coming Friday. The freezer was empty, the trash was outside ready for the weekly pick up, and our few things were packed and ready to go. I kept patting my pockets to make sure my toll money was where it needed to be, ready to get us off the peninsula. Then Paula's phone rang on Tuesday afternoon. It was Pete. From his tone, we knew it was bad news straight away.

"I need another week, maybe two. The house isn't going to be ready for you I'm afraid. The heating won't be working so we can't let you stay in the house."

We listened to him while we looked at each other. We both shook our heads. Enough was enough. For once, apparently, even Pete had to admit that it was indeed as bad, perhaps a little worse than it looked.

"Listen, Pete, we love you to bits man. But here's the thing, we *are* leaving Jim's place on Friday morning. We *will* be arriving in Somerton on Friday afternoon and moving into the house that same day."

And we hung up.

And Finally...

As soon as we hung up, we immediately felt terrible. I called Jim and explained our situation. Jim was losing revenue on his rental house, we had been in it for two seemingly endless months rather than the two or three weeks estimated and, while he was as kind as usual, it was clear he wanted us out too. We discussed giving Pete another week, but I felt, as lovely as he was to deal with, if we gave him a week, he would take another, and perhaps another, and...well if you have stuck with this sad little tale this long, you know as well as I do what would happen.

Knowing that the end was finally upon us, the weight of uncertainty was lifted and we started to enjoy our walks again. We traipsed up the Minnadhu, the great grassy promontory that rolls steeply down to the rocks. We walked between the old trees that created a creepy tunnel of ancient foliage. Storm Eunice had loosened the soil and vast roots reared out of the chalky ground. We didn't linger, there were clear signs of a previous landslide and it was only a matter of time before another one swept a few of these trees, and perhaps a passing rambler or two, over the cliff edge and into the crashing waves beneath us. Every walk was a farewell to the sights, the glittering expanse of the sound across to Plymouth, the iron-grey warships churning the water into white plumes as they performed maneuvers, and the sounds, the constant crashing boom of waves on splintering rocks and the cries of the seabirds that circled the skies above us.

We ate a few meals at the Halfway Inn and enjoyed the massive log fire that the Landlord played with on a nightly basis. We ate the last tin of beans from the larder and the few remaining eggs from the fridge. And then our final morning arrived. We lugged the rest of our crap down to the car park at the bottom of the hill and with another apology to Pi and Archie, tucked the dogs away onto their beds suffocatingly hemmed in by a wall of coats and wellies, bags, and shoes.

We turned the corner out of the car park, gave one wistful look back at the shop that sold the incredible pasties and we roared up the narrow, steep hill for the last time before we met something coming down the hill in the opposite direction. We crossed the Tamar twenty minutes later and I threw my two-pound coins into the toll station with an almost sexual abandon, like a pair of dirty old lady knickers hurled onto stage at a Tom Jones concert.

We took our time on the return journey, we wanted to give Pete as much time as we could, as if we believed that thirty or forty minutes at the end of an eight-month build might any difference. We parked the Mini on the road outside the build and walked up the access road. Pete had clearly been lying in wait for us and met us before we could even get close to the house. He looked pale and stricken with worry and already had his hands out of his donkey jacket in supplication as he approached us.

"Look, look, when you see the house, you have to believe me, it's not as bad as it looks, honest to God."

Since Pete's phone call, we had steeled ourselves for arriving at a house still partly open to the elements, without running water or even heating.

"It's OK Pete. We forced the timeline; we will deal with it. How much did you manage to get done?"

Oh, quite a lot, but I really don't want you to be angry and disappointed."

"Does it have water and electricity?"

"Oh, sure."

"Heating?"

"Oh, sure."

Paula and I looked at each other, both confused and a little relieved. We shrugged.

"Then it sounds great. What didn't get finished?"

"Well, the painters are still in there and the chippies need to finish a few jobs. I just don't want you to see it and be really angry. There is still no garden by the way."

"We really didn't expect there to be one Pete. We are good with that. Can we see it?"

"Oh, sure, sure."

We walked through the mud that might one day become our garden. A few solitary fence posts stood like broken teeth, still to be cemented in their holes. But the house looked amazing. The Tri-fold doors stood open and the laminate flooring was covered in muddy shoe prints where the trades had been rushing, in and out, trying to finish last-minute jobs, but to our eyes the house was finally, eventually, thankfully done.

Carpets were down, bathrooms shone chrome and white tile, and the kitchen sparkled under its still protective film coating. We flicked switches that were installed in the walls and lights that hung from actual ceilings blinked on, we turned handles on windows, windows actually secured to the building, and they opened and closed. Taps issued water in both hot and cold variants, radiators radiated, cookers cooked, freezers froze, and fridges...cooled things. It was all amazing.

Some closet doors were propped on painter's cloths waiting for a second coat, and there were some patches on the walls that the painters were still working on, but nothing whatsoever for us to complain about.

We shook Pete's hand and thanked him for his efforts. He gave me a hand moving in a bedframe and a mattress that we had stored in the garage. And there was the couch we had ordered all of those months ago in Reading, so we set that up in the lounge. I put some of the packing cardboard down on the laminate floors so the trades didn't have to worry too much about wiping and taking off shoes. While me and Pete busied ourselves, Paula did a run in the Mini to our storage container in Curry Rivel to pile as many of our boxes, the ones containing mugs and kettles, toasters, and cutlery as she was able. I got the WIFI working and the TV turned on, we made a brew and we sat down on our new couch to wait for the trades to fuck off home and leave us in peace for the night.

And, just like that, after months of planning and moving and upsetting the puppers and stressing ourselves, we were done. Once fully moved in, the house took longer to completely finish than we anticipated. The garden in particular wasn't finished for another month or so. Jim, as always, was tremendous and didn't ask us to close and pay until we were happy, so we essentially lived rent-free while it was all being wrapped up.

The house was both smaller and larger than we had anticipated. The downstairs floor plan is just three small open plan rooms, kitchen into dining room and dining room into lounge. Whatever pots and pans drum solo I am performing in the kitchen Paula also gets to enjoy, and you might as well just go ahead and pause live TV and take a paracetamol or three when the kitchen garbage disposal is doing its job, but otherwise it's fine. Upstairs by contrast goes onward and upward. Three stories make the master bedroom a climb too far so we chose the middle floor to sleep on.

The lawn got laid to thick turf and once nicely greened, the dogs turned it into a patchy brown tundra. We emptied the storage locker and I was genuinely sorry to say farewell, it was lovely play-acting our own little episode of Storage Wars every time we visited. I would be Jarrod and Paula would play Brandi. We just needed a Dave Hester to shout "YUUPP!" from the sidelines.

Well, we settled quickly into the house and back into village life. It was lovely having a permanent home again, surrounded by things that we had chosen and purchased. We had a few books, but no bookshelves, but our kitchen drawers contained our pots and pans, cutlery, and plates and dishes. We spent several weeks assembling brand new flat pack furniture and then picked up the clothes that had been stored on the floor and placed them in drawers that were actually ours. We had a drawer in one of the downstairs storage units for important paperwork, bills passports, and such, and, like normal people, we set aside a large drawer in order to slowly accumulate odds and ends like sellotape, stamps, takeaway menus, and paperclips—the 'rubbish drawer'.

Archie and Pi relaxed into their routine, breakfast, walk in the countryside, nap for five hours, dinner and a late afternoon walk around town, then collapse on the sofa to cuddle up and watch us watch nonsense on the TV—bliss. The dogs adore life in the UK. There are oodles of off-leash walks down long muddy lanes. There are sheep and cows in the fields, deer running wild, hens and foxes.

That should be the end of the story. It's certainly a good, even a fairly happy ending. The poor dogs certainly deserve such a thing. But having become who we are, after just over three months we put the house on the market and sold it. Archie is rolling his eyes at me as I type this. He can't quite believe we are about to be on the move again. But here is the thing. We want something more to do. Having settled to live in England, and with all of our imposed traveling done with we became bored.

To generate maximum fodder for further writing, the options slimmed down to me becoming a large animal vet, or Paula and I buying and running a Bed & Breakfast together. Even though James Herriot has proved time and time again that having your arm rammed, shoulder deep, up a cow's arse pays dividends in book and TV royalties, it takes six long, hard years to become a vet, so we ruled that one out.

We figured that there should be tons of weird encounters and stupid anecdotes I could steal from deranged guests in the hospitality industry, particularly for somebody as aggressively inhospitable as myself. We figured we would make the ideal couple to be candidates for the next Basil and Sybil Fawlty and even looked at a place in Torquay. We haven't found the right place yet but keep following the journey to see where we end up. I'm certainly intrigued, as I hope you are.

Thank you so much for the read—it is genuinely appreciated. If you enjoyed the tale, it would be very kind of you to leave a review on your favorite bookstore.

Please take a moment to visit my website to see more books and get great discounts and offers.

You can find me at www.andycwareing.com

ANDY C WAREING

Read the next books in the series:
WE'RE ON OUR WAY

MISTAKES WERE MADE

ANDY C WAREING

Andy is a multi-genre Indie author, originally from the United Kingdom. He has lived with his wife Paula and their two dogs Archie and Pi in Atlanta GA for the last fifteen years (with the exception of a year in Spain/UK during the pandemic). At heart always British, he loved living in the U.S.A but will never vocalize the American pronunciations of basil, banana, or tomato. He currently lives in leafy Somerset, land of apples, cider, and weather so perpetually wet, 'wellies' are considered formal wear.

Please take a moment to visit my website to see more books and get great discounts and offers.

You can find me at www.andycwareing.com

<u>ANDY C WAREING</u>

Be a stalker and follow me on Facebook, Goodreads, or my author page on Amazon for updates on new projects:

facebook.com/andycwareing

goodreads.com/author/show/21017809.Andy_C_Wareing

amazon.com/author/andycwareing

email: author@andycwareing.com

Made in United States
North Haven, CT
02 March 2024

49462190R00075